RUNNING THE GAUNTLET

TRANSITIONING INTO A NEW LEADERSHIP ROLE IN HIGHER ED

MARIA THOMPSON, PH.D.
SUSAN C. TURELL, PH.D.

ACADEMIC IMPRESSIONS | 2021
DENVER, CO

Published by Academic Impressions.

CR Mrig Company. 5299 DTC Blvd., Ste. 1400. Greenwood Village, CO 80111.

Copyright © 2021 Maria Thompson and Susan C. Turell.

Cover design by Brady Stanton.

All rights reserved.

No part of this book may be reproduced, or stored in a retrieval system, or transmitted in any form or by any means, electronic, mechanical, photocopying, recording, or otherwise, without express written permission of the publisher.

For reproduction, distribution, or copy permissions, or to order additional copies, please contact the Academic Impressions office at 720.488.6800 or visit:

www.academicimpressions.com

Academic Impressions

ISBN 978-1-948658-18-8

Printed in the United States of America.

ANOTHER BOOK YOU MAY ENJOY

Empowered: Leadership Development for Higher Education

Get C. Clinton Sidle's new 360-page developmental guide to four leadership masteries. The only book of its kind, *Empowered* is designed as a text for in-house leadership development programs in higher education, packed with tools, techniques, and activities for developing leaders.

https://www.academicimpressions.com/product/empowered/

"Clint Sidle's new book takes us on a journey of exploration of both the art of leadership and the practice of personal understanding. Believing that we cannot effectively lead others until we understand ourselves, Clint provides a generous array of exercises designed to help participants discover who they are and how they are prepared to lead. *Empowered Leadership* suggests leadership is not about having the right tools and skillsets; it is instead, a spiritual practice in which we must commit to learn, listen, grow, reflect, and synthesize." – *Allison M. Vaillancourt, Ph.D., Vice President, Business Affairs & Human Resources, University of Arizona*

"'Could you imagine what Cornell would be like if everyone took this class?' These are the words of an undergraduate student profoundly affected by Clint Sidle's leadership course. Having helped support the faculty leadership program and student course at Cornell University, I have read many such extraordinary testimonials and evaluations… *Empowered* provides the theory and the roadmap for all of us to find fulfillment and a greater purpose, and to be effective leaders in higher education. Sidle offers guidance for individuals as well as those facilitating leadership programs. Given the increasing fragility of the world around us, empowered leaders who inspire the human spirit are needed like never before. *Empowered* is a must-read for everyone." – *Mike Hoffmann, Professor Emeritus, past Associate Dean and Director, College of Agriculture and Life Sciences, Cornell University*

CONTENTS

PREFACE 1

SECTION ONE: YOUR RELAY LEG 4

SECTION TWO: POWER DYNAMICS 42

SECTION THREE: RELATIONSHIP BUILDING 108

SECTION FOUR: TEAM BUILDING 165

SECTION FIVE: ESSENTIALS OF SHARED GOVERNANCE 199

SECTION SIX: OPERATING ESSENTIALS 255

SECTION SEVEN: PULLING IT ALL TOGETHER 284

APPENDIX: CAST OF CHARACTERS AT JACKSON ROCKGROVE UNIVERSITY 379

ABOUT THE AUTHORS 385

PREFACE

How to Use This Workbook

You have probably attended generic leadership workshops that provide you with a lot of ideas in the areas of leadership theories, leadership styles, networking, change management, time management, and other related topics, but they do so without discussion of your skills and experience. Other workshops will help you focus on you and your skills and experience, which are important; however, you are just one part of a multifaceted landscape that determines success.

The approach of this workbook is to embed practical information and self-reflection in a framework that helps you assess the intersection of the macro and micro context in which you will lead. Self-knowledge and practical skills are important, but they exist and are applied within a context. Context is everything. This workbook will help answer the question, "How do you use practical information and knowledge of your skills and experiences to be a successful leader within a given context?"

The purpose of this workbook is to help you create your own unique roadmap for your first three to six months in your new leadership role. Based on our experiences, leaders new to their roles have very little time to lay a strong foundation for their tenure. Much like a sprint relay, your time in the role is short—and it is dependent on the history you inherit. Don't squander this precious time at the start; once you accept your new position, be prepared to 'hit the ground running' from the moment you begin, and to use your brief honeymoon period to create the greatest possibility of success. This workbook will provide you with a process that, once completed, will result in the creation of your own unique three- to six-month roadmap.

Whether you are starting a new position at a different institution or are being promoted internally, determining how to approach the numerous challenges and opportunities presented to you can be overwhelming. If the thought of tackling all of the material in this workbook seems daunting, the assessments of the macro and micro context, self-reflection questions, case studies, and activities can be bundled in a variety of ways to create learning capsules customized to meet your needs, interests, and schedule. Additionally, the micro context questions can be used to help job seekers scan and assess an institution during the interview process. Further, assessing the intersection of the macro and micro context can aid you in setting goals and developing plans for your unit/institution. Finally, different sections may become more salient as duties expand or leadership roles grow or change, so you can use this workbook over time.

Each section provides some broad considerations and key concepts. We ask you to then spend some time reflecting. Be honest and candid with yourself, as these answers will provide some important foundations for the unique roadmap you will develop at the end of the workbook. We also provide some case studies to illustrate situations that you may encounter. (Please refer to the Appendix for a description of Jackson Rockgrove

University and the cast of characters you will encounter in these case studies.) Finally, we provide some questions that, once answered, will create a working document that you can use even before Day One.

This workbook is organized into seven sections. As we developed the ideas for this workbook and reflected on our time spent in higher education leadership, we found that there are two organizing categories to help with effectiveness: *people* and *processes*. Of course, these overlap significantly, because people design and work within processes. Even so, some of the sections will focus more on working with people as the most important resources, and others will focus more on the use of good processes. Lastly, as we reflected on leadership, we also wanted this workbook to move from ideas to application—that is, to aid in your creation of a unique planning tool, or roadmap, for your individual situation—for your leg of the relay.

You will find that six of the sections expand on the two categories of people and processes, and we will describe each section in a bit more detail below. If you want to focus more on people, you may want to start with Sections Two, Three, and Four. If you are interested in processes, Sections Five and Six may be useful. Section One provides an overall framework, and Section Seven, once completed, will result in your unique plan, created by and for yourself.

We use the metaphor of a sprint relay race to describe time spent in a senior leadership role. **Section One** introduces you to this model and the parallels this metaphor provides. Research tells us that the time spent in any leadership role is decreasing, which creates a need for an efficient and effective start. Perhaps counterintuitively, it is also the time to begin thinking about your legacy even before or as you assume the role. And, as in a relay race, you are part of a team, which includes what you inherit from your predecessor and the context of the institution in which you will be working. This initial section will help you to prepare for your time in the role, offering an overview from start to finish, from the time of receipt to the handoff of the baton.

Section Two explores the power dynamics of leadership roles, sometimes referred to as "politics." The nature of power dynamics is that they exist both interpersonally and institutionally. This workbook, and Section Two in particular, examines both, as well as the intersection of the two. Interpersonal power dynamics are inherent to and permeate leadership. We will examine both how to be aware of and how to manage these dynamics in order to be effective—including how to handle boundaries, both up and down the reporting structure. Some leadership development focuses only on the interpersonal. This section goes beyond that, and takes a deeper dive into how climate, institutional norms, and power dynamics will impact your leadership, and how these factors will need to be assessed quickly. Embedded in these are equity and inclusion considerations, which are introduced in this section and then woven in further throughout the workbook.

Once you examine the power dynamics of Section Two, **Section Three** will expand on the *people* aspects of leadership. This section concentrates on developing mostly one-on-one relationships. You will likely be building relationships with both internal and external constituents. Identifying important constituents early in your leadership leg of the race will help you to cultivate important relationships. Given the existing power dynamics, this section also explores developing others' trust in you and determining whom you can trust. Shared governance is increasingly important, and this section elaborates on how to best utilize it to accomplish your goals for your unit and for the campus as a whole.

Section Four examines building teams. Sometimes your unit and the institution will have all the talent required; other times, talent will need to be cultivated or developed. This section will explore assessment of existing talent, and how to create it where there are gaps. Professional development can be expensive in both time and money, so this section looks at both targeting what is needed and how to provide it effectively. The effectiveness and usefulness of work done in committees and task forces is greatly affected by team membership, so this section also provides guidance on building these groups, in addition to those elected by shared governance.

Understanding shared governance is essential to effective higher education leadership. **Section Five** investigates the underlying processes for engaging in shared governance processes effectively. Using a data-supported decision-making model assumes the availability of trustworthy and transparent data. This data must include the budget, both revenue and expenses, and how resources are allocated. The ability to conduct continuous improvement depends on assessment of student learning, and evaluation of programs through accreditations or other methods. These processes are covered in this section, along with delving into each as they specifically intersect with shared governance processes.

Section Six concludes the sections focused on process by examining operating essentials. These include communication strategies, both daily and in crisis; how to review and update policies and practices; and finally, coming full circle, your initial hopes for your time in the position. As you prepare to leave your current leadership role, this section asks you to revisit the hopes and plans you acknowledged in Section One, at the beginning of your part of the relay. As you prepare to hand off the baton to your successor, Section Six helps you to consider what your likely legacy will be.

Finally, **Section Seven** will assist you as you combine and synthesize your work in the other sections. As you compile the tasks you identified on the various roadmap worksheets embedded in Sections One through Six, you will see that there is more to do than is humanly possible, especially in the probable short time frame of your acclimation and orientation to the role. This section will help you to see all possible issues in the aggregate and will reinforce the need to be realistic in setting goals. It will also help you to pick the most important tasks to accomplish in the first six months. This is crucial to good self-care and will enable you to be more effectively focused in your work. It will also be a good reference for you to revisit every six months in order to reassess—to omit items that are not important or urgent, and to add others you might have missed. The unique roadmap you create can serve as an organizing touchstone for your entire leg of the race, from receiving to passing the baton, and will increase your likelihood of winning that gold medal.

SECTION ONE: YOUR RELAY LEG

1. Leadership: The New Reality – The Track and Field Analogy
2. Inheritance: The Gift That Keeps Giving
3. Setting the Stage for Your Legacy (First Thoughts)

Whether you are starting a new position at a different institution or being promoted internally, determining how to approach the numerous challenges and opportunities presented to you can be overwhelming. In this section, you will be introduced to the sprint relay model of leadership in higher education and how it can be used to frame your approach to the first three to six months in your role. This section also guides you in handling inherited issues, especially those that are personnel-related.

Section One concludes by focusing your attention on laying the foundation of your legacy by setting realistic stretch goals for your unit/institution while making a healthy work-life balance a priority.

1.1. Leadership: The New Reality—The Track and Field Analogy

> KEY CONCEPTS AND CONSIDERATIONS
>
> - A relay sprint as the paradigm.
> - It takes effort to shift your perspective.

Sprint relays are a good analogy for senior leadership positions in higher education. In both cases, you spend years preparing to achieve your personal best so that you will be ready to succeed when presented with an opportunity to accomplish your goals. Once the moment arrives, there is limited time to grasp the (leadership) baton, which is handed to you in a blind position. Baton in hand, you accelerate to achieve top speed. Fumble the baton and you will lose time; drop the baton and you will be disqualified. The competition is fierce and there are factors, such as the setting and external conditions, that are out of your control. To complicate matters, the time frame for executing this complex set of variables grows shorter and shorter; the years of tenure in leadership roles are becoming shorter, just as the time lengths of sprint relays are becoming shorter.

SECTION ONE: YOUR RELAY LEG

Macro Context: Setting and Conditions for the Race

Just as the altitude, wind speed, and temperature impact a runner's performance, the setting and conditions in the macro context will impact the issues you will face as a campus leader. Technology, politics, demographics, and other aspects of the external operating environment create the macro setting and the conditions under which you will lead. This macro context for higher education is created by 21st century megatrends such as the following:

- Social media literally allows millions of people to discuss and shape the narrative of your institution's internal issues.

- The 24-hour news cycle, fed by social media, leads to judgments made in the court of public opinion before you are able to take the time to assess a situation in a comprehensive manner using your official policies, processes, and shared governance mechanisms.

- The interrelated changes in the distribution of age, race and ethnicity, and income in the U.S. have major impacts on enrollment. To stabilize or increase enrollment, leaders must consider responding by:
    - appealing to older students with a different portfolio of academic offerings in flexible modalities,
    - creating a safe and welcoming environment to attract and retain BIPOC students, and
    - offering more student financial aid to serve greater numbers of lower-income students who may ordinarily be priced out of attending college.

The COVID-19 pandemic has disrupted in-person higher-ed operations by driving many campus functions to take place remotely. The revenue model, designed to support salaries and other operational costs, is not only dependent on tuition from courses, but also on revenue from fees associated with facilities use, athletic events, parking, and dining and residence halls at full capacity.

Micro Context: The Baton and Exchange Zone

In a 400-meter relay, the baton is passed in a 20-meter segment of track called the exchange zone. This limited area for receiving or passing the baton tests the skill and speed of a runner. Passing the baton before entering the zone or receiving the baton after leaving the zone results in disqualification. Likewise, drop the baton and you will be eliminated from the race. Therefore, a successful baton exchange requires a great deal of attentiveness and can determine the outcome of the race. A race run by relay teams of equal speed will be won by the team that executes better in the exchange zone by having the ability to pass and receive the baton smoothly while running at top speed. Sprint relays are won or lost in the exchange zone.

The baton for a leader in higher education is the internal environment, or micro context, that is being "passed" to you. The micro context is created by the people, processes, and situations at an institution. The exchange zone is the first three to six months in your position—a critical time in a leader's tenure to get a firm grasp on the micro context and accelerate to top speed. The micro context is determined by Carnegie classification, organizational structure, financial situation, location, and the mission and history of the institution. Additionally, public or private control, being part of a university system, unionized employees, and enrollment trends are other factors that can shape the micro context of your campus.

Successfully operating in a micro context is the focal point of this workbook, and in each section, we will present content regarding the people and process dimensions that comprise this micro context.

Sprint Relay as Paradigm

When you begin your new position, you will *not* be handed a blank slate on which you can paint an idyllic vision of the perfect unit, using your favorite palette of colors. Instead, you will inherit an existing set of problems that may have been years or even decades in the making. Gone are the days of the ceremonial leader who primarily holds a position for the sake of maintaining a hierarchy or to shake hands and take pictures with students at a ceremony. You are not just holding a title. There is real work to be done and complex problems to be addressed as early and as quickly as possible. The problems senior leaders face are becoming more complex and, statistically, senior leaders are serving in their positions for shorter and shorter time periods.[1]

You must continually be aware of the macro and micro context in which you operate, and you must make intentional, and often difficult, decisions to make progress. Also, be aware that many of the factors shaping the micro context on your campus may be beyond your control, and you nevertheless must find ways to be an effective leader, developing strategies that consider your limitations. As senior leaders in a new paradigm, we must shift to a new perspective. We do not aim just to get and keep a job; we shift our perspectives to achieving success with integrity. Just know, up front, that this will be very challenging at times, will require your courage, and it will probably make you unpopular with some people. Going into a new position with the awareness that you will face complex issues within a macro and micro context will aid in your success.

Resistance to These Realities

Typically, most people in higher education are more able to accept the external macro realities than to acknowledge the micro context changes to leadership in higher education. "Most people," in this case, may include ourselves or those we work with, or both. We acknowledge the passage of time and its impact on technology, politics, demographics, and economic conditions, but the traditions, hierarchies, and bureaucracy unique to colleges and universities seem to be carved in stone. Therefore, it is tempting for some senior leaders to believe that the situation at their institution is impervious to shifts in the macro environment, and that their institution is a standalone entity shielded from the winds of change due to the unassailable virtues of post-secondary education. But as part of the global ecosystem, colleges and universities are inextricably linked to the macro context, as evidenced by the disruption of business models and the destabilization of enrollment currently

---

[1] See the American Council on Education's *American College President Study* (www.aceacps.org) and the Council of Independent Colleges' *A Study of Chief Academic Officers at Independent Colleges and Universities, 2009-2019*.

SECTION ONE: YOUR RELAY LEG

taking place. These and other changes in the macro environment are causing an industry-wide existential crisis, which inevitably alters the micro environment and shifts the paradigm for higher education leadership.

In some cases, unwillingness to acknowledge the realities of the sprint relay paradigm can be driven by high salaries, egos, and a perceived lack of comparable options. Some senior leaders, even when they know the daunting challenges they face in their positions, will find themselves reflecting on the following questions as they contemplate the end of their tenure: How else could I make this much money? Who am I without my position and title and the perks that go with them? I worked so hard to get where I am; how could I leave this position, even if I am tired and stressed out?

These are difficult times for higher education, and the road ahead is uncertain.

> **We wholeheartedly believe that it is better to know the realities than to pretend that they don't impact you and your institution.**

The sprint relay paradigm allows you to approach positions as a 'longer-term' interim, knowing that your time to pass the baton will most likely occur more quickly than your predecessor's. And if your leg of the race is longer than most, this approach will help you keep from acquiescing to the pressures to maintain the status quo. This will allow for a more informed approach that enables you to do the hard work and make difficult or unpopular decisions with integrity, keeping the long-term health of the institution in the forefront of your thinking and actions.

MICROCONTEXT

What is the microcontext at your institution related to the following?

Institution type	(e.g., state-controlled or part of a university system vs. private; two-year vs. four-year; comprehensive, liberal arts, research, land-grant, flagship, etc.)

Organizational structure of campus	
Budget situation	
Geographic location	(urban/rural; what kind of competition: other institutions; population trends)
Unionized or not?	
Missions and history of the institution	

SECTION ONE: YOUR RELAY LEG

SELF-REFLECTION

How long have you been in your current position? How long were your predecessors in the role? What are your thoughts about the length of time you have served to date? Too long? Not long enough? Just right?

What do you notice is uncomfortable for you about this sprint-relay model of leadership?

What might contribute to possible resistance to working within the model?

How long do you expect to be in your current/next leadership position?

SECTION ONE: YOUR RELAY LEG

Are there factors that influence the likelihood of playing it safe just to keep a job, versus making difficult and unpopular decisions/actions to do the job with integrity?

ROADMAP 1.1

Identify strategies to overcome any resistance to ideas that might ultimately benefit your success in this leadership role.

1.2. Inheritance: The Gift That Keeps Giving

"You kick the can down the road, (but) you will get the can again." —Joe Thorndike

> KEY CONCEPTS AND CONSIDERATIONS
>
> - Face difficult, inherited personnel issues directly.
> - Set realistic stretch goals for the institution/unit that can be accomplished in three to five years.

After experiencing the pride and excitement of being promoted, relatively early in your tenure you will notice problems not mentioned during the interview process. These issues were most likely omitted for a few reasons:

1. The hiring authority is not aware of the issues,
2. the hiring authority is not aware of the *severity* of the issues,
3. the issues are not a priority from the hiring authority's perspective,
4. the issues have grown since your interview, or
5. the campus community wants you to have a good impression of them and didn't want to "air dirty laundry."

Also, keep in mind that everything cannot be covered or uncovered during the interview process. When you are interviewing, consider this a qualifying race for the actual sprint relay. You can get a snapshot of the institution by studying their website or reading the position prospectus, and you can begin your inquiry during the interview and during the period before you arrive on a new campus. Ultimately, the only way to know what you are dealing with is to ask probing questions and collect and review as much data as possible after you arrive on a new campus.

Inherited problems, especially those that are personnel-related, can consume a good deal of your time and derail your efforts to move your unit/institution forward. You may want to avoid personnel problems or try to wish them away, but they will not likely go away on their own—it is more likely that they will get worse. Since employees have seen administrators come and go, some people will just 'wait you out'—knowing they will be in their job longer than you will be in yours. Therefore, they do not think it is necessary to move out of their comfort zone and change what they are doing. Remember that you are coming into a new position with energy and excitement while they likely have been slogging through some of the same institutional issues for years, seeing very little change other than the names and faces of administrators. Also, while you were being interviewed about the changes your supervisors will expect you to make to move the institution/unit forward, no one is having the equivalent discussion with your new reports; your reports are most likely assuming that transformational change is above their pay grade and is your responsibility, not theirs. They have found a way to cope with any dysfunction and limits of the campus culture.

There is a method of dealing with personnel issues that we do not recommend. Do not avoid dealing with underperformance or behavioral problems by creating what is called the roving employee. We have all seen an underperforming or difficult-to-get-along-with person who is moved from unit to unit and their performance and behavior never improves because it is never directly addressed. The person is just moved or allowed to rove from unit to unit across the university. This rarely resolves the problem. It is the coward's way out, and it is not fair to the employee or the unit that must take them in and endure them until they are moved to the next unit, to continue underperforming or causing drama and chaos.

When taking a new leadership role, begin by determining if there are any performance issues with your direct reports and other key personnel in your unit. They are the people you depend on to accomplish your unit's goals and objectives. Also, others will be looking with interest to see if you hold your own team accountable or if you let them get away with poor performance or unprofessional behavior. Be careful not to single people out but conduct data gathering as an equitable process. Make sure to gather and review both qualitative and quantitative data.

If there are faculty or staff performance problems, you should delegate these issues as much as possible and set a deadline for completion to avoid dragging the issue out unnecessarily. Require your delegate (or yourself) to gather multiple data points, and keep in mind that performance evaluations will offer limited utility due to people's difficulty in conducting accurate evaluations. Keep in mind that tenured faculty may not be reviewed if a post-tenure process is not required. Also, it is not unusual that employees in an underperforming unit will be rated as satisfactory or above. This is the Lake Wobegon effect—everyone is above average. If improvement is needed, performance evaluations should be used but may not be effective due to a flawed instrument and/or because it is difficult for people to give good formative feedback. Reorganization can be a less direct way to remove someone from the institution or a specific role (e.g., department chair) but can be time consuming and may, in some instances, require cabinet-level or board approval. Set a precedent for future reviews by communicating expectations early, even during the interview process. This is important so we'll repeat it: Communicate expectations early. This means you need to be clear about just what your expectations are. Finally, shared governance plays a role in the evaluation process, especially for faculty. There may even be a formal mechanism for shared governance bodies to evaluate the performance of administrators.

If you inherit faculty issues with promotion and tenure decisions, determine if it is a matter of uneven application of standards, or if there are problematic policies and practices, or a combination of both. If you are handling your first rank and tenure review in your new role, become thoroughly familiar with the policies and process to avoid stepping on any landmines; this can be very easy to do if you happen to go against the decision of the rank and tenure committee during your first review in your new role. An opposing decision on the matter of rank/promotion is usually less contentious than opposing tenure. In either case, follow your institution's policy regarding follow-up meetings with the committee. If allowed, meet with them to discuss both your data analysis and theirs to explain your decision. Have HR and university counsel review any written documents to the committee or candidate to protect the institution, and yourself.

Campus hierarchies can impact inherited staff issues. Whereas there is a well-established career ladder for faculty, this is not always the case for staff positions. The relative ease or difficulty of being promoted as staff can greatly influence the culture of the campus. Internal promotions for staff may be possible up to a point, generally to the level of middle management. Senior-level positions, however, tend to involve a national recruitment process that may eliminate internal staff from serious consideration. Be aware that this can result in frustration, disengagement, and varying degrees of active or passive sabotage from the staff you inherit.

As a campus leader you will be expected to champion diversity, equity, and inclusion (DEI) to help create a safe and welcoming environment for students and colleagues. Make it a priority to uncover and address long-lived biases as part of culture, such as sexism, racism, and homophobia. You must make unambiguous statements of your commitment to DEI in your written and verbal communications. Call out offending behavior you encounter in meetings, and meet with offenders individually to address their behavior. To do so, you must also make a commitment to continually deepen your own learning and growth about DEI. We will discuss this later in the workbook.

Review your institution's/unit's policies to determine their impact on people of different races, sexual orientations, or religions. It will be easier to use and validate quantitative data than qualitative data, but both are necessary to describe the reality of your institution's environment. For quantitative data, analyze patterns of pay by comparing women to men and people of color to white people. Also, examine the percentage at rank for faculty and level for staff between and among these groups. Qualitative data can be captured through climate surveys. Climate surveys can be difficult to conduct, but an experienced consulting firm can administer a reliable instrument and help determine a baseline for your campus.

Later in this section, you can explore these ideas further in four case studies:

- The Case of the Roving Employee
- The Case of the Jolly Dean
- The Case of the Premature Promotion
- The Case of the Back-peddling (Or Is It Back-stabbing?) Tenure Appointment

Section One: Your Relay Leg

MICROCONTEXT

1	What personnel matters are you inheriting?
2	What are the policies that apply to personnel?
3	What is your role, and what is the role of HR regarding personnel matters?

4	What performance evaluations are used, if any?
5	Who are you hearing about already, whose actions are visibly problematic?
6	Who is invisible to you in the first 6 months? (That is, who is not engaged?)

7 | Are there faculty or staff performance problems?

Can you delegate these issues and set a deadline for resolution? If so, list the issues and the responsible delegate:

Issue   *Delegate*   *Deadline*

_____   _____   _____

_____   _____   _____

_____   _____   _____

_____   _____   _____

_____   _____   _____

_____   _____   _____

8	Are there issues with promotion and tenure decisions? If so, is it a matter of uneven application of standards, or are there problematic policies and practices, or both?
9	What is the role of shared governance?
10	What hierarchies exist at your institution (e.g., faculty in relation to staff)?

Section One: Your Relay Leg

11   Do existing or proposed policies have different impacts on different groups of people?

12   How are international students, faculty, and staff treated on your campus?

13   Does the living/learning environment support the success of students, faculty, and staff with differing abilities? Are appropriate and adequate resources in place to address their needs inside and outside the classroom?

SELF-REFLECTION
Did you inherit difficult personnel issues you would like to avoid? If so, why?
Are *you* really committed to creating an inclusive and equitable campus? Where are areas that you hold privilege/power over others? How can you develop the skills and attitudes to be inclusive and equitable more of the time?

Section One: Your Relay Leg

If you are involved in personnel reviews in your role, what will you do if you uncover someone who has not earned rank/tenure, or a positive review? What if you have to go against a shared governance committee or their supervisor? How might it impact your decision if their supervisor is someone who reports to you, or not?

When you uncover inequities such as sexism, racism, and homophobia, will your own embodiment impact this and seem self-serving? Do you get bonus points for being an ally, if not part of a group?

ROADMAP 1.2
First, √ Assemble qualitative and quantitative data needed to review performance of direct reports, faculty, and staff. Then:
Develop *(a)* a list of your performance expectations for your team and *(b)* strategies to communicate these performance expectations effectively:

Section One: Your Relay Leg

Refer back to the work you did in Item 8 in the *Microcontext* on page 18. Prioritize and develop strategies for inherited personnel issues, including timeline for completion, and responsibly delegate:

Articulate your understanding and commitment to equity and inclusion:

List methods to communicate your expectations and commitment to equity/inclusion, and how you will reinforce them over time:

Delineate which policies/practices need revision first to help the institution (or your area) become more equitable/inclusive:

Section One: Your Relay Leg

Do you have a plan to uncover and address long-lived biases as part of culture (sexism, racism, and homophobia)? Please describe or develop a rough outline of your plan:

Describe the plan to address any issues related to xenophobia:

Case Studies

1. THE CASE OF THE ROVING EMPLOYEE

Frankie Fiscal has been promoted to campus CFO after working in the business and finance division for several years. Frankie is thrilled to be promoted, and life is good until Frankie realizes that Drew Drama has just been transferred to the CFO's office. The outgoing CFO, who had already signed retirement papers, agreed to take Drew from another unit where the unit head complained bitterly about Drew's poor performance and the constant turmoil created by Drew's behavior.

Frankie is all too familiar with Drew, who has moved from one unit to another for years with no improvement in performance or temperament. A few of Drew's supervisors have tried to address Drew's performance and behavior, including attempts to separate Drew from the university. Each supervisor would meet with the Director of Human Resources, Mona Volador, and leave the meeting cautiously optimistic that they might receive assistance with the situation. But eventually, after meeting with President Petry, Mona would hold a second meeting with the supervisor and inform the supervisor that they have no memory of offering to support them with corrective actions or separation. Mona, who conveniently never takes notes at meetings they attend, ultimately suggests that the best course of action is to look for a "better fit" for Drew in another unit.

Frankie begins the new position on a Monday, and by Wednesday it is clear that Drew will not work out. Frankie meets with Mona to discuss options, leaving the meeting with some hope, but Frankie's hopes are dashed during the second meeting with Mona. The only relief Mona can offer Frankie is assistance with transferring Drew to another office. To make matters worse, Frankie learns from a colleague in the advancement division that Drew is related to Big Bucks Bentley, an alum, board member, and major donor, who is in the process of establishing another multimillion-dollar endowment.

Feeling trapped, Frankie suddenly sees a way out when Newby Nelson, the administrator recently hired to head a newly combined enrollment management and student affairs unit, mentions to Frankie a need for more employees in the new unit. Frankie offers to "help" Newby by transferring Drew to Newby's unit to save time on the university's cumbersome and lengthy hiring process.

As you complete case studies in this book, you can refer to the Appendix for a glossary of the characters.

Section One: Your Relay Leg

CONSIDER:

What should Frankie and Newby discuss before the transfer takes place? What are potential ways this issue could be managed successfully if Drew is transferred? What should Frankie do if Drew stays in the CFO's office?

What genders and ethnicities did you imagine about these characters? (How) do any of your answers change based on their intersectional genders and ethnicities, in relation to other characters?

2. The Case of the Jolly Dean

Provost Earnest starts their new leadership role with several direct reports, and in getting to know them, notices that one of them, Dean Jolly, talks a good game and never delivers. Dean Jolly is well-liked and always joking; however, one of the departments under them consistently reports some of the lowest pass rates for licensure in the state, which is resulting in decreasing enrollments in that program. The dean takes no responsibility for those pass rates. This is just the tip of the iceberg. Curricular initiatives are stalled; personnel matters in their College fester. The provost realizes that they need to either remove Jolly as dean or develop a corrective action plan.

CONSIDER:

What does Provost Earnest need to consider to reach a decision? What steps might one take for either course of action?

What genders and ethnicities did you imagine about these characters? (How) do any of your answers change based on their intersectional genders and ethnicities, in relation to other characters?

3. THE CASE OF THE PREMATURE PROMOTION

Provost Earnest receives a recommendation to promote a faculty member (or staff) from the review committee of their peers. As each recommendation is read, it is clear that they ignored some important information that contradicts granting promotion at this time. The provost cannot in good faith recommend promotion during this cycle. The person can submit for promotion again the following semester or year—and has time to address the deficits in their performance.

CONSIDER:

In what processes should the provost engage? To whom should they speak and how might they frame the issues?

What genders and ethnicities did you imagine about these characters? (How) do any of your answers change based on their intersectional genders and ethnicities, in relation to other characters?

4. The Case of the Backpedaling (Or is it Back-stabbing?) Tenure Appointment

Dean Wink, for three years prior to Professor Combative's tenure application, has carefully crafted responses to all personnel processes regarding them, and has carefully noted all areas needed for improvement for a successful tenure bid. Combative submits their tenure portfolio, which gets mixed support from their department; further, they are not recommended from the shared governance Rank and Tenure committee. Dean Wink concurs that there are significant gaps in the record and does not recommend tenure to Provost Earnest, who concurs. However, President Petry decides to grant tenure; Dean Wink suspects this is motivated by a desire to avoid conflict.

CONSIDER:

What dynamic does this create for Dean Wink regarding future tenure recommendations? What are the implications for this department and their colleagues? Should Dean Wink address this with anyone and if so, what might they say/hope to accomplish?

What genders and ethnicities did you imagine about these characters? (How) do any of your answers change based on their intersectional genders and ethnicities, in relation to other characters?

1.3. Setting the Stage for Your Legacy—Establishing Realistic Goals and Achieving Work-Life Balance

> KEY CONCEPTS AND CONSIDERATIONS:
>
> - You are not your role.
>
> - Take time for regular self-care.

At some point, it will be your turn to hand off the leadership baton to someone else, and that time may be sooner rather than later. Given that you will not be in your leadership role forever, it is healthy to learn to separate yourself from your role from the start. Even though you are spending long hours and lots of mental and emotional energy to do your job, you should not allow it to define you and you should be careful to not believe your own press. Some leaders become so full of themselves that they develop hubris, a characteristic that detracts from being an effective leader—as feeding their ego becomes the focal point rather than student success and the well-being of the institution. Thinking you know best—even if you *do*—can short-circuit getting important information to improve any decision. You need to remain objective to execute your job properly and to guard your mental, emotional, and physical health. Take your job seriously and do your best, but do not let the work consume you. Try to establish a healthy work-life balance from the outset.

The sprint relay leadership model takes into account the decreasing tenure of senior leaders and acknowledges the constraints of the macro and micro environments and the tremendous challenges created by their confluence. For example, in spring 2020 the COVID-19 pandemic left no campus unscathed as in-person courses transitioned online, and as all but a few employees worked remotely, upending well-established operating practices. Enrollments plummeted on many campuses in fall 2020, further destabilizing the traditional business model, which was already being disrupted by technology and demographics. At the same time, the tense racial climate and polarization in American politics has colleges and universities grappling with their own climate issues as students question the inclusivity of the curriculum and the dearth of people of color on the faculty and in leadership. Challenges of this magnitude require senior leaders to focus their limited time and resources on seemingly unlimited problems.

It is imperative to place high priority on goals that can create an environment where you and your colleagues can be productive, and where students and the institution can flourish. Recognize that what is considered a priority will differ depending on the constituency groups. Board members, lawmakers, alumni, and donors can demand your time and attention and often have a different view of institutional priorities. This can put senior leaders in a double bind where internal constituencies, students, faculty, and staff will have a different view of your role and responsibilities than the governing board, lawmakers, and other external groups. Both groups, internal and external, tend to judge your commitment and performance based on their perception of how much time you spend directly engaging them and their issues relative to other constituency groups. Despite your best efforts, you will not likely be able to solve every problem you encounter, accomplish every goal you set, or please every stakeholder.

At the start of your new leadership position, you have the best opportunity to lay the foundation for the legacy you will leave when your time in that role is over. While you may be tempted with a long list of possibilities, more often the impactful initiatives will be few in number—maybe three to five.

> **Therefore, establish a limited number of meaningful and measurable goals that put the long-term health of the institution/unit front and center.**

Set boundaries and separate from your work daily. Schedule time for self-care and vacations (or staycations). Set your mind free from the cares and worries of your job when not in the office (or your home office).

Later in this section, you can explore these ideas further in a case study and an activity:

- The Case of Catch-22
- Activity: Search for the 10th President of Jackson Rockgrove University

MICROCONTEXT

1	Given fiscal and human resources, inherited challenges, and the external operating environment, what are realistic stretch goals for the institution/unit that can be accomplished in 3 to 5 years?

SECTION ONE: YOUR RELAY LEG

SELF-REFLECTION
How are you NOT your role?
How can you stay grounded and keep hubris to a minimum?

Going into your new leadership role, what do you hope is your legacy, at least the top three items?

What are you doing to lay the groundwork to create that legacy?

SECTION ONE: YOUR RELAY LEG

ROADMAP 1.3

Develop and prioritize realistic stretch goals tied to vision and taking into consideration inherited issues. (See *Microcontext* above.)

Identify and schedule self-care activities:

Activity	When

Identify coaching and support groups for your leadership journey:

Case Study and Activity

Consider the following case study and activity to explore these ideas further.

THE CASE OF CATCH-22

Dr. Monkson receives an unexpected call to meet with the provost. Surprisingly, Monkson is being asked to serve as interim dean for a year. Dean Wink is leaving for a provost position at another institution on June 30, and Monkson, if they accept the assignment, will become interim dean effective July 1. The search for a new dean will commence during the interim period and the provost informs Monkson that they will be eligible to apply for the permanent position, if desired. The provost is giving Monkson until the end of the week to give an answer.

Leadership Agenda for Interim Dean:

- Complete a program prioritization process—make final decisions regarding the disposition of red (elimination), orange (has one year to improve with possible elimination pending), and yellow (has three years to improve with possible elimination pending) departments. Reallocate resources, including faculty lines, after finalizing decisions regarding which departments to close, merge, or invest in (green category departments).

- Investigate new plagiarism allegations against Harper Hustle made by Monkson's former housemate, Blake, a postdoc in the research institute. To complicate matters, Hustle filed a sexual harassment complaint against Blake a few days after the new plagiarism allegations. The interim dean will have to

Section One: Your Relay Leg

work with the EEOC office and the research compliance office to resolve both issues. See *The Case of the Research Hustle* on page 106.

- Meet with angry faculty members in Pat Pompous's department who are threatening a vote of no confidence against them. They have informed the outgoing dean that if they are not satisfied with the interim dean's handling of the situation, they will file a complaint against the interim dean and recommend to the provost that that person be barred from applying for the permanent position.

- Due to a conflict Monkson's department had with the marketing department regarding the name of a new academic program, there are no marketing activities for the new academic program. The enrollment for the new program has 90% fewer students than originally projected in the market demand study using the rejected program name. The interim dean will have to decide whether to overrule the faculty's decision not to use the name suggested in the marketing department's study or to put the program on the red list for potential closure.

Although relatively early in their career, Monkson thinks the interim position may be a good opportunity to try on the leadership hat but has reservations after reviewing the issues that need to be addressed.

CONSIDER:

List the issues facing Monkson. Rank their priority of importance to manage/resolve, and note the timeframe needed for each resolution.

Priority   Issue   Timeframe to resolve

_____   _____   _____

_____   _____   _____

_____   _____   _____

_____   _____   _____

_____   _____   _____

_____   _____   _____

_____   _____   _____

If Monkson takes the position, what steps might they take to manage/resolve each of these?

Can Monkson delegate any of these issues, and if so, to whom?

Are there any issues that Monkson can/should ignore? If so, what are the potential consequences?

Section One: Your Relay Leg

Activity: Search for the 10th President of Jackson Rockgrove University

Review the job announcement for the presidency of Jackson Rockgrove University, below, and respond to the questions following it. (You may also wish to review the JRU mission and values in the Appendix.)

Job Announcement

The Board of Trustees of Jackson Rockgrove University (JRU) is seeking nominations and applications for the position of president. The new president will succeed President Petry, who will retire in July after an illustrious 35-year career in higher education.

Responsibilities and Opportunities for the Next President

The president is the chief executive officer of the University, reports to the Board of Trustees, and is expected to embody the values and advance the mission of JRU. The president is responsible for the vision and strategic leadership of all university operations and carries out the policies of the JRU Board.

The next president will lead JRU through the challenges and opportunities facing postsecondary education institutions since the advent of the COVID-19 pandemic.

- Create an entrepreneurial environment where innovations in teaching and learning and revenue generation are complementary activities.

- Increase enrollment of new students by expanding target markets and reinvigorating the academic enterprise with a focus on multiple modalities, new credential options, and new, high-demand academic programs.

- Raise retention and graduation rates of returning cohorts by focusing on student success-centered policies and practices in all units of the institution.

- Strengthen the fiscal health of the institution and build new revenue streams to support current operations and to fund new, strategic projects.

- Foster an environment of collegiality and cooperation by building a common vision for the university.

- Champion diversity, equity, and inclusion, and create a welcoming environment for all members of the campus community.

- Strengthen the intercollegiate athletics program to focus on the academic performance and well-being of student-athletes while building a tradition of winning at the conference level.

- Advocate and serve as an ambassador for the university across the state and the nation to build strong relationships with influential organizations and individuals who can enhance the JRU brand.

- Leverage the university's standing as an anchor institution and 'steward of place' to help overcome losses experienced in the wake of the pandemic in surrounding communities.

- Build an atmosphere of trust and transparency, and demonstrate a respect for the principles of shared governance.

- Create a state-of-the-art living/learning environment by updating the university's facilities and technology infrastructure.

- Significantly increase the endowment and lead JRU's 100th anniversary celebration capital campaign.

Preferred Skills, Experiences, and Characteristics:

- An earned doctorate from an accredited institution.
- 10 or more years of successful senior leadership experience in higher education.
- Distinguished record of teaching, research/creative scholarship, and service.
- Demonstrated commitment to the values held by the university.
- Commitment to diversity, equity and inclusion for all members of the university community.
- Experience creating new revenue streams that build on existing institutional strengths.
- Demonstrated success leading change while honoring history and tradition.
- Successful record of increasing enrollment and improving student success metrics.
- Experience addressing human resource issues effectively.
- Excellent oral and written communication skills and experience interfacing with varied constituencies.
- Strong fiscal acumen with experience in resource reallocation.
- Proven record in fundraising, relationship building, and advocating to external constituencies.
- Demonstrated experience using data-supporting decision making to achieve institutional priorities.
- Commitment to openness, transparency, and shared governance.
- Experience leading successful accreditations and strategic planning initiatives.

CONSIDER:

What questions come up for you as you read this position description? Do you see possible red flags?

Section One: Your Relay Leg

What else would you want to be sure to ask about, prior to applying for the job?

Given what you know about the campus from the job description, what are some potential areas for the next president's legacy?

SECTION TWO: POWER DYNAMICS

1. Navigating the Political Landscape and Power Dynamics
2. Climate, Gossip, Campus Lore, and Misinformation
3. Setting Boundaries

Section Two focuses on power dynamics that frame the political aspect of your work as a leader. The personal is always influenced by the political, and neither the environment in which you work, nor the interpersonal relationships themselves, are neutral.

In this section, you will learn how to increase your awareness of these power dynamics. Whether or not you ever make them explicit in your interactions, as you engage with this section, you will raise your awareness of the ubiquitous nature of power dynamics—and translate your awareness to improve interactions and avoid pitfalls due to the inherent inequities.

2.1. Navigating the Political Landscape and Power Dynamics

> **KEY CONCEPTS AND CONSIDERATIONS**
>
> - Power = hierarchy. Control over who defines the 'norms,' whose 'reality' is considered as the right way or the only way.
>
> - Learn the political landscape and power dynamics as quickly as possible.
>
> - Discover and utilize the culture to accomplish your goals.
>
> - Power dynamics are always operating. Influence can be minimal or big, but it will be there.
>
> - Some power is positional: the role people are in, within a hierarchy.
>
> - Some power is based more on personality or influence. This is less visible and takes a bit of time to suss out.

SECTION TWO: POWER DYNAMICS

Every campus has politics, and power dynamics define politics. In this case, power means 'control over,' whether structurally (e.g., who supervises whom) or in other, less obvious ways. Some power is positional: the role people are in, within a hierarchy. Some power is based more on personality or influence. This is less visible and takes a bit of time to suss out.

Sometimes institutions will pretend that they are more egalitarian than they really are—and will try to minimize the influence of politics. This is rooted in the belief that power is a bad thing.

> **Power over others exists. It is not inherently good or bad. How one uses it can be for good or for bad, and that can create both/either good or bad outcomes.**

Controlling via power doesn't work well; marginalizing people is hurtful. But to pretend that power hierarchies do not exist just lets the negative effects occur unchecked.

We must acknowledge that power dynamics are always operating. Their influence can be minimal or substantial, and they always exist. And power is embedded in a hierarchy. Much as we might not like this, some people have more power to make decisions than others. Some people have more power to make decisions that impact a larger number of people than others. And sometimes, that power is used to control others, and to keep the hierarchy in place.

When we consider their embodied or lived experiences, some people (White, male, rich, straight, educated) have more power based on societal institutional norms, reinforced by racism, sexism, homophobia, classism, and other biases. In these cases, marginalization of others and its negative consequences are likely, intended or not. In these cases, power dynamics will mean hurtful control over others, intended or not, as those who have power define the norms. Their 'reality' is considered as the right way or the only way, and these norms are embedded in the policies and practices of the institution. We will discuss this further below, in Section 2.2: *Climate, Gossip, Campus Lore, and Misinformation.*

Heavy stuff, right? So, take a deep breath, and remember that while power dynamics exist, it's better to be aware of them than to pretend they don't.

Let's start with how you can evaluate and gather data about the power dynamics of the institution and your new role. Start with *you* in your leadership role, and then look at where you are in the hierarchy/vertical reporting lines.

Examine the organizational chart. Look over the reporting lines. Note how reporting structures may affect who speaks up in meetings (or not) when supervisors or folks with power are in the room. As you attend meetings, make mental notes of these dynamics.

Your own power will be influenced by your predecessor. Remember that you are being handed a baton, as part of the relay race. Part of that baton is the history and relationship of the institution to that role and the person in your role prior. They will still be an influence on your time in the role, especially at the beginning.

You are inheriting the campus's relationship to your role. Some people on campus respect the role, others do not. And sometimes, even if the role is respected, you might want to determine if it's respected begrudgingly, or sincerely. For example, do you hear people state deference to the role only but with no respect for knowledge or experience? This may occur in comments such as, "We don't agree, but the president says we have to." This is an example of begrudging respect, rather than respect rooted in a true understanding of the role and in the experience and knowledge one has in it.

The Predecessor

More specific to your situation is the relationship of the campus to the person who was last in your role. (If you are in a newly created role on campus, good for you! This may not apply to you just now.) Related to this, there are some specific factors that will impact you more directly:

- Is your predecessor still on campus?
- If so, how vocal and well respected are they?
- If they are no longer on campus, do you know the circumstances of their leaving the role?

Whether physically on campus or not, they may have a lingering influence, like the smell of perfume after someone has left the room. You might want to find out who their champions on campus are. Most people in leadership have networks, and those often last after they leave the role and/or institution.

Whether or not they are still on campus, you will also want to assess if they were well liked. If they were well loved, you may be in a no-win situation. Sometimes history is rewritten, and they become saviors after their departure, even if they were hated while there. If they didn't hold others accountable, it's a no-win situation. Setting limits will make it harder for you to be liked, so try for respect. Be sure to be as transparent as possible, within the limits of confidentiality. One of us found ourselves having to make a hard decision, and saying no to a department about a hire, following predecessors who had never said no. While the departmental faculty members were angry and vocal, we had built enough respect in the role that other faculty leaders wrote an unsolicited letter on our behalf supporting our right to make the decision, with credibility for our experience and knowledge.

Later in this section, you can explore these ideas further in three case studies:

- The Case of the Rebound Girlfriend Dean
- The Case of the Little Provost Who Could
- The Case of the Previous Provost's Promise

Sometimes, there is no predecessor. If you are in a founding role, you may be able to set some of the norms for the role. If so, set norms regarding your expectations for self and others. Communicate those through words and actions. We will discuss this further below in Section 2.3: *Setting Boundaries*.

Opinion Leaders

If only organizational charts told the whole story of power! But they don't. There are informal power dynamics at every institution. We will refer to the people who hold this informal power as *opinion leaders*.

How can you determine who the opinion leaders are? You can observe relational networks. When people gather for meetings, who sits with whom? Who eats lunch together? If you have access to social media, which people are Facebook friends?

If you have a role in formal personnel processes, such as promotions or tenure, note who writes letters of recommendation for each other. If hiring from within, note who is writing letters of recommendation. If there are award processes, note who writes letters of support.

Both co-authors of this workbook have had roles in personnel review. It's been interesting to see how letters of recommendation vary. Some folks only use peers, rather than their colleagues who are at the next higher level. We were often able to see friendship groups emerge in mutual letter-writing—groups that were never visible publicly on campus.

What *is* visible are the dynamics in meetings. A clue about opinion leaders can emerge as you observe who speaks out against the majority of their colleagues. Who is not afraid to challenge peers or say something that may not be popular? Does the room get quiet when certain people speak? Whose comments often spark more conversation?

At one meeting, there was a rousing discussion of the need for tiny enrollment caps for online courses. Even though the faculty in the meeting had the research about course caps in online classes and learning effectiveness, the conversation was rapidly coalescing on a recommendation of very few students per course. That is, until one senior faculty member who teaches many online courses spoke up. They noted that they had taught courses at various enrollments, and that they concurred with the literature. That is, learning effectiveness varied based on student level (e.g., undergrad or graduate), and topic, among other variables.

You may also figure out power by what the constituencies value. For example, campuses that value research may hold prolific researchers in high regard just based on that. Their influence extends beyond their actual expertise and accomplishments.

At one campus, a faculty member had an international reputation as a researcher, but was not involved in any meaningful way in shared governance. Yet, they were still held in great esteem, and when they spoke about any topic, their opinion held weight.

Another campus we know was truly student-centered. Two sentences into any meeting with a topic related to learning in any way, student perspectives were brought up. This was not the case in any other campus in which we worked.

Lastly, notice who does not speak up but uses behind-the-scenes relationships to influence. These types of opinion leaders can be difficult to deal with if obstructionist.

Later in this section, you can explore these ideas further in three case studies:

- The Case of the Faculty Award Gang
- The Case of Dean Lackey
- The Case of Tricky Dick

MICROCONTEXT

1	What does the mission and founding of the institution tell you about the historical norms that underlie policy and practice? As much as possible, identify those norms:

Section Two: Power Dynamics

2 | What is valued by the institution? Research? Teaching? Is it nominal only, or is there evidence that it's *really* valued?

3 | What are the political footballs in your unit or institution?

| 4 | To examine power dynamics, you might want to note: Who has control over whom? Regarding what functions or areas? Who is subordinate to you? |

| 5 | What are you inheriting that your predecessor 'gifted' to your unit or to the institution? |

Section Two: Power Dynamics

6 | Who has won awards?

7 | Which meetings are productive, and which are theatre?

SELF-REFLECTION
What power dynamics are operating for you currently, both nominally and informally (embodied)?
Revisit your reflections about sexism, racism, homophobia, etc., from your self-reflection in Section 1.2, and consider your location within each identity impacted. As you think about power dynamics, what additional ideas might you note about how these operate at any university, and about your role to challenge them?

Section Two: Power Dynamics

Think about times in the past when you felt free to speak up or didn't feel free to speak up. What power dynamics were occurring?

What has to be in place to make a meeting productive?

How have you or can you contribute to make meetings more productive?

ROADMAP 2.1

Where are the places or events where you might observe informal relationships or power dynamics among people/constituents?

Section Two: Power Dynamics

What are your plans to create opportunities for observation?

Develop a plan to use Facebook and other social media to learn about people and relationships at the institution:

Case Studies

1. THE CASE OF THE REBOUND GIRLFRIEND DEAN

Dean Outsider's immediate predecessor, Dean Perfect, has stepped back into another role on campus. Perfect was well loved while in that role, and in every meeting during Outsider's first 100 days, someone will ask "What would Dean Perfect do?" or reference their work. Dean Outsider realizes that they are like a 'rebound girlfriend'—they'll never live up to the 'one that got away.' Dean Perfect really is a decent person and does not appear to be fueling this dynamic on campus.

> CONSIDER:
>
> Can Dean Outsider establish their own reputation? If not, why not? If so, how might they stop the comparisons?
>
> How might Dean Outsider deal with references to Dean Perfect in meetings?

Section Two: Power Dynamics

Should Dean Outsider involve Dean Perfect? If so, how and about what?

What genders and ethnicities did you imagine about these characters? (How) do any of your answers change based on their intersectional genders and ethnicities, in relation to other characters?

2. THE CASE OF "THE LITTLE PROVOST WHO COULD"

Former Provost Pretentious, who was in the role about a decade before the current Provost Earnest, envisioned the glory of being an R-1 institution, even though they worked at a regional comprehensive of about 4000 students at the time. Their parting gift was a reduction from a 12 credit/semester teaching load to a 9 credit/semester teaching load, so that the faculty could produce more scholarship. The faculty did not like Provost Pretentious while they were there, but this one decision is upheld as their wonderful legacy. Looking at data, Provost Earnest sees a sizable increase in budget for hiring adjuncts in the past decade, although there has been a significant decline in enrollments and no appreciable increase in scholarship production. The provost brings up revisiting faculty workload at a meeting with all the deans, who express great concern over this possibility.

CONSIDER:

What problems did Provost Pretentious inadvertently create?

Noting what Provost Earnest inherited, do they have any options to adjust this situation? If Provost Earnest was asked to reduce budget expenditures, is this adjunct workload policy/practice something they could tackle? What are the pros and cons of doing so? If Earnest decided to try and correct this, what might be some areas to approach or activities to do?

What genders and ethnicities did you imagine about these characters? (How) do any of your answers change based on their intersectional genders and ethnicities, in relation to other characters?

3. The Case of the Previous President's Promise

President Paternal retires after leading the institution for 25 years. They invite incoming President Petry to attend their farewell speech to the campus, where they will hand off the keys to their office. Petry accepts the invitation and looks forward to taking the helm the day after President Paternal's farewell speech. At the end of the speech, President Paternal promises a 10% raise to all employees and receives a 10-minute standing ovation. This unexpected statement hits the incoming president like a blunt object given that the institution is already barely making ends meet financially.

President Petry spends the first several weeks on the job scrambling to figure out a way to make good on the previous president's promise. Afraid to disappoint the campus and end the honeymoon period, President Petry announces to the campus that the pay increase will be implemented over a period of 3 years. Most members of the campus are satisfied with this plan and the president's popularity is secured. A large number of employees make long-term financial commitments based on receiving an increase over time while others pass up opportunities at other universities.

Although it was a struggle, the increase was implemented in years one and two by tapping into the reserve fund and deferring a number of facilities and technology upgrades. Unfortunately, the third year of the plan coincides with the COVID-19 pandemic and a significant enrollment downturn. Petry is panicked by the institution's financial situation and is not sure how to maintain operations *and* implement the third year of the pay increase, as the reserve fund is perilously low and tuition revenue is far below the projected amount. The president's popularity has taken a few hits and there has been occasional chatter of a vote of no confidence, but it always dies down after announcing the continuation of the pay increase plan each year.

CONSIDER:

Should President Petry:

_____ Complete the last installment of the pay increase for all employees?

_____ Complete the last installment of the pay increase for some employees and defer for others?

_____ Cancel the last installment of the pay increase for all employees?

_____ Defer the last installment for all employees?

_____ Other:

What genders and ethnicities did you imagine about these characters? (How) do any of your answers change based on their intersectional genders and ethnicities, in relation to other characters?

SECTION TWO: POWER DYNAMICS

4. THE CASE OF THE FACULTY/STAFF AWARDS GANG

Stevie Staff is asked to serve on a selection committee to recommend faculty and staff to system-wide prestigious awards, which are competitive within and among system campuses. The committee receives a packet of nomination materials for each nominee, and their job is to advance one recommendation per award from their campus. They may also decide to *not* recommend if no one meets the criteria. Stevie notices in year two of their service on this committee that the same people nominate each other for these awards, and that those who serve on the selection committee have nominated their friends. They also notice that often the nominees do not meet the minimum criteria for awards.

CONSIDER:

What can/should Stevie do? Would the possible actions change if Stevie were faculty? An administrator?

What genders and ethnicities did you imagine about these characters? (How) do any of your answers change based on their intersectional genders and ethnicities, in relation to other characters?

---

5. The Case of Dean Lackey

Provost Earnest is reviewing the tenure file for a faculty member and notes that Dean Lackey has written a glowing letter of support. The faculty member is not part of Dean Lackey's College. The provost also notices that the faculty member is good friends with many faculty in Dean Lackey's College. A quick glance on Facebook indicates that Dean Lackey is Facebook friends with this group as well.

> CONSIDER:
>
> What issues, if any, might this letter raise? Is there anything that Provost Earnest might need to do/address, and with whom?
>
>
>
> What genders and ethnicities did you imagine about these characters? (How) do any of your answers change based on their intersectional genders and ethnicities, in relation to other characters?

SECTION TWO: POWER DYNAMICS

6. THE CASE OF TRICKY DICK

Provost Earnest is tasked with developing new majors on campus that align with job trends in the area. The provost worked with faculty in one department over a year, and the curriculum they wrote for a professional degree was sent to the shared governance curriculum committee last week for consideration. Provost Earnest has noticed that in the past, the curriculum committee is fairly lax; however, this major was unexpectedly voted down. Provost Earnest finds out that Tricky Dick, a faculty member in History, convinced their fellow History faculty colleague on the curriculum committee, Trusting Taylor, to stall this major, citing the decline of respect for liberal education. Further, they told Taylor that the development of the major was a ploy to create a job for the provost's spouse, who has a doctorate in that discipline. (While the doctorate is true, Provost Earnest's spouse is not interested in working at this institution and is happily employed elsewhere.)

CONSIDER:

What political/power dynamics are present here? (How) should Provost Earnest deal with each/any of them?

Should Provost Earnest address Tricky Dick directly? Why or why not? If so, how?

What genders and ethnicities did you imagine about these characters? (How) do any of your answers change based on their intersectional genders and ethnicities, in relation to other characters?

2.2. Climate, Gossip, Campus Lore, and Misinformation

> **KEY CONCEPTS AND CONSIDERATIONS**
>
> - Even with the optimal structures and policies in place, climate and culture will override them.
>
> - Racism, sexism, classism, and heterosexism are embedded in all campuses, but may be manifested in unique ways in your institution's culture.
>
> - Learn the political landscape and power dynamics as quickly as possible.
>
> - Discover and utilize the culture to accomplish your goals.

So far, we've discussed power dynamics that operate mainly between and among individuals. However, at the meta-level, power dynamics manifest through your institution's policies and practices, and are supported by larger societal norms. These norms validate the experiences of people who are white, male, heterosexual, able-bodied, have a higher socioeconomic status, etc. Conversely, those who do not fit this 'mythical norm' (Audre Lorde, 1984)[2] often find themselves invalidated, ignored, invisible, and marginalized. We all must acknowledge and keep in the front of our minds that racism, sexism, classism, and heterosexism are embedded in all campuses, but may manifest in unique ways.

This section will help you to explore both the meta-power dynamics and how they likely impact the local campus climate and culture. Also, each campus will have its own unique ways in which these power dynamics impact groups, and you will want to explore these unique aspects to your institution, while keeping in mind the encompassing societal-level influences. Even with the optimal structures and policies in place, climate and culture will override those structures and policies.

You will want to learn the political landscape and power dynamics as quickly as possible, starting to assess them even during your interview process. Once you accept your new position, you will want to discover and utilize the culture intentionally to accomplish your goals.

---

[2] See Audre Lorde's *Sister Outsider: Essays and Speeches*. Crossing Press, 2007.

Campus Lore

Let's start at the university/institution level. Learning the unique flavor of your campus climate and culture is important.

Every campus has its own lore. Sometimes campus culture is framed as mission. That is, while institutions have their formal mission, there is often informal talk *about* mission that is shorthand for how the employees think of themselves and the institution. Sometimes the reality does not match the perception, and in such cases, the lore might be used to maintain a climate and culture that is rooted in keeping things the way they were in the past.

For example, one of us worked with a faculty salary negotiating committee. While the faculty often spoke of how committed the institution was to a social justice mission, when discussing salary increases, members reverted to the previous, inequitable way of calculating raises. The new formula would advantage any employee making $60,000 or less, and disadvantage those making more than $60,000. Some faculty members claimed that the formula just couldn't change that quickly and that faculty needed time to get used to the new, more equitable formula. Does this sound like aligning actions with the mission? Yet if you asked any faculty member, they would tell you, to the person, that the institution, and they as employees, were committed to social justice.

As you start in your new position, listen carefully. Belief in the lore can override the reality. Lore gives you insight as to the climate and culture of the institution and can also make it difficult to shift that culture.

Students are often a topic that is ripe for campus lore. The student of yesteryear is often referred to as smarter, less fragile, more mentally healthy, and more motivated. The perceived disconnect between the student who is admitted and who *should* be admitted can be another way to assess assumptions about the institution and the perceived culture.

Gossip

Gossip is another way in which culture and climate are maintained. Gossip—knowing the inside scoop—can be a source of power for some people who like to spread it. Notice whether or not people who listen to it choose to believe the gossip they hear rather than their impressions about actual interactions.

While we would like to believe that most people assign greater credibility to their firsthand interactions and experiences than to the gossip, unfortunately we have found that to be the exception, not the rule. Even if you act with integrity and transparency, others may choose to believe what they hear from others at second or thirdhand, rather than their own eyes and ears in their actual experiences of you.

Misinformation

Misinformation is a special type of communication that creates the climate and culture on a campus. In spite of your most careful and clear communications, often you will hear information that is not based on data. That disconnect can be quantitative—such as when campus constituencies disagree with or don't want to believe the data—or qualitative, a misinterpretation of what was said. (We discuss data-informed decision making in detail in Section Five.)

Note how misinformation is used at the institution, and how it impacts the culture of data use and the level of mistrust. Does it help or hurt progress? Misinformation is not only used to obstruct ideas. Sometimes proponents of an idea will only provide partial information that is beneficial to their desired goal. They may leave out information that they think will be a barrier to your agreement. Listen carefully so that you can ask questions to fill in omitted, but important, details that you may need.

If you hear misinformation, note whose agenda it serves. Don't assume that it's intentional. Please assume good intentions unless proven otherwise. (You can also ask that people assume good intentions on your part, as well!) Sometimes anxiety over change makes it hard for people to hear information correctly.

We have found it interesting that so many times, highly educated people at universities—who are trained in analytical and critical thinking—start with questioning the validity of the data when it supports ideas that may challenge the status quo, as in cases like an examination of program prioritization, workload models, or enrollment trends. Yet, these educated individuals will also readily accept statements made by colleagues that rightly fall under opinion rather than a data-informed statement.

If your institution seems to have an abundance of misinformation, you can counteract it by use of data. Be sure to include assumptions and sources. You may need to share the data numerous times.

Later in this section, you can explore these ideas further in two case studies:

- The Case of the Harvard of the Southeast
- The Case of the Dickensian Departments

Campus Climate

Campus climate covers a lot of territory. Typically, the term refers to how welcoming and inclusive the institution is regarding gender and ethnicity. It can also refer to the norms of the particular institution.

Let's start with issues related to gender and ethnicity. Unless you work at an Historically Black College or University (HBCU) or a Hispanic Serving Institution (HSI), your university is built on a legacy that includes a white norm. Most institutions are also built on a male, heterosexual, middle/upper class, able-bodied norm. Audre Lorde referred to this as the 'mythical norm.' This legacy is mostly invisible, and it advantages the people who are part of the normed group and disadvantages those who are not.

Take a moment to reflect on your own relationship to privilege and power, or lack thereof—your own intersecting identities. This is important to your growth and understanding about diversity, equity, and inclusion (DEI) and to your ability as a senior leader to infuse DEI in the campus climate. What is your gender, ethnicity, sexual orientation, class status? As we talk about areas where you have privilege, do you feel defensive? Guilty? Shame? Excitement? As you consider your varied identities, probably you fall into the normed group some of the time, and at other times, you experience marginalization.

Institutional history means that these norms and inequities are embedded in policies and practices, and are likely invisible to most, except to those who are impacted or excluded. For example, most universities have a policy about stopping the tenure clock. It *appears* gender-neutral. However, women are more likely to use this policy, given disproportionate family obligations. If tenure committees look down on people who stop the tenure clock, then women are disadvantaged disproportionately. A second example involves age—one of us worked recently at a campus that decided to reduce the institutional contribution to retirement. Although it was implemented across all employees, it inadvertently impacted the older employees more—those who were nearing retirement.

Each campus also has its unique climate. One of us worked at a campus in the Midwest where the work ethic was high. Emails on weekends and evenings were the norm; it was not unusual for fall semester grades to be due after Christmas. This was in stark contrast to another campus in which no committees met during December or May, even though the semesters ended at the typical times. Factors related to power dynamics that are unique to your campus climate may also impact relationships between faculty, staff, and administrators, how things get done, transparency, the use of data, and almost every facet of work on campus.

Climate surveys inquiring about inclusivity concerning gender and ethnicity, if done well, are very expensive. They typically assess the lived experiences of employees and students. It is very difficult for these to be done well internally; therefore, many institutions hire external consultants. If you decide you need a climate survey, decide how you will use the data *and use it!* Too many campuses do these surveys and then never use the results to effect change. And do not do a climate survey unless it's done well. A poorly done survey creates an illusion of effort but reinforces the inequities. For example, if the survey questions focus on descriptive data about marginalized and underserved populations, the results and conclusions drawn may inadvertently blame them for lack of achievement. This will mask the institutional barriers that create an inequitable environment, allowing these barriers to continue unchecked, unexamined, and unmodified.

Besides a climate survey, you can also gather secondary data to learn more about the campus climate related to these issues. Notice patterns related to personnel matters; it's fairly easy to get a snapshot of equity related to ethnicity and gender. You can ask for data analysis of salary or retention by race, sex, and rank. If you notice inequities, this suggests that racism and sexism are part of the campus climate—and that *systemic* racism and sexism are part of the campus climate. Their effect will extend to how the institution's policies and processes are interpreted and implemented.

What are the patterns of hiring and/or people leaving the institution? What are the reasons given for not hiring BIPOC candidates? Does the institution follow best practices for hiring, reducing the possibility of bias? (For example, at regional comprehensives, all too often we have seen that search committees hire only people they know. In smaller communities, relatives are given special consideration for jobs.) Similarly, do BIPOC faculty and staff leave in greater proportions than white faculty and staff?

The Overall Culture

It is possible to conduct data analyses related to the climate and equity—but how can you discover the unique overall culture of an institution? We have found it useful to notice disconnects between typical processes at places you worked before and those where you work now. Anything that appears unique at your new institution may be an area to focus on to uncover hidden climate or culture issues.

There may be other areas that also provide shortcuts to assess the overall climate. Notice whether peers hold each other accountable. Are there 'sacred cows' that others say can't be changed? Listen for people saying (even implicitly): "We don't do that here." "We tried it and it didn't work." "We always…" "We never…" All of these can help you suss out the unique climate of the institution.

You can also read past minutes of shared governance bodies, and note the topics that were raised (or that were *not* raised). What is the tone of these minutes? Do these bodies even keep minutes? You can also talk to opinion leaders on campus. Who they are and what they choose to focus on can help you learn about the climate, via informal culture/power dynamics. Are all the opinion leaders male and white? If so, this may be a clue about racism and sexism at work. Are they all from one College? That tells you what discipline(s) are valued at that institution.

Later in this section, you can explore these ideas further in three case studies:

- The Case of the Invisible Inequities
- The Case of the Missing Hair Salons
- The Case of the Homespun Hires

MICROCONTEXT

1	Do you know how the campus truly views your role? If so, how do they view it?

2 | What were the circumstances under which your predecessor left the role? Who are their champions and devotees? Did your predecessor hold others accountable?

3 | Misinformation is a special type of communication that creates the climate/culture on a campus. What misinformation have you heard already? Whose agenda does it serve? Note how it is used. Does it help or hurt progress?

Section Two: Power Dynamics

4 | How has 'mission' been used to perpetuate 'lore' at institutions where you have served in the past?

How is mission used to perpetuate campus lore at your current institution?

5 | What are the 'sacred cows' that others say can't be changed?

6 | What does the personnel data suggest about equity on the campus concerning BIPOC? Women? Look at both hiring data and at those who leave. What do you notice?

Section Two: Power Dynamics

7 | What are the reasons given for *not* hiring BIPOC, or for BIPOC leaving the campus?

8 | Are women paid equitably compared to men? What are the gender percentages at each rank? What about BIPOC, compared to white staff?

| 9 | What is revealed by a data analysis of salary or retention by race, sex, or rank? |

| 10 | How are international students, faculty, and staff treated on your campus? |

Section Two: Power Dynamics

11 | Does the institution follow best practices for hiring and performance evaluations?

12 | Do existing or proposed policies have different impacts on different groups of people? Who do these policies benefit? Who is unintentionally harmed?

SELF-REFLECTION

Who have you known at any workplace who has gossiped? What was your reaction to hearing others' gossip? What were the observable power dynamics?

When have *you* gossiped?

Section Two: Power Dynamics

Think about times in the past when you felt free to speak up, or when you didn't feel free to speak up. What power dynamics were occurring?

Think about a time you heard something that you found out wasn't true. Who did this misinformation serve? What was its purpose? What did you do when you found out it wasn't true, and how did that impact your relationship to the person who shared the misinformation?

When you list your own intersecting identities, how do you respond emotionally to this list? Defensive? Guilt? Shame? Anger? Excitement?

Are there disconnects between how things typically operate at places you have worked previously versus where you are now? (If the processes are unique to your current institution, these may be areas to focus on to uncover hidden climate or culture issues.)

SECTION TWO: POWER DYNAMICS

ROADMAP 2.2

First,

√ Read past minutes of shared governance bodies to help you discover the campus culture.

Then:

How are you going to learn the lived mission at the institution? Where will you look for clues?

If you know of any areas of misunderstanding at the institution, what data will you gather to correct it and how will you communicate the findings?

What processes do you want to implement to set norms for your newly formed area?

Section Two: Power Dynamics

Who will you talk to about power dynamics on campus to assess them? What's your plan? Include how you will identify opinion leaders, given the informal power they hold at the institution.

List ways to uncover and address long-lived biases that have become part of the campus culture (sexism, racism, homophobia, xenophobia, etc.).

Review the data you gathered in the *Microcontext* above. Examine patterns of hiring and/or people leaving the institution (e.g., look for lack of equity by race, sex, etc.), including an analysis of whether or not BIPOC leave in greater proportions. (If the institution is not hiring qualified BIPOC proportionately, uncover the reasons given by search committees/hiring managers.)

Does your institution/unit provide appropriate and adequate resources to support the success of students, faculty, and staff with differing abilities? If not, determine ways to address their needs.

Section Two: Power Dynamics

If the data you gathered in the microcontext above yields inequities, how will you begin to address them? What is the timeframe for these actions? What is realistic? What foundation needs to be laid first?

Case Studies

1. THE CASE OF THE HARVARD OF THE SOUTHEAST

Dean Outsider, when new to their previous job at a two-year institution which offers AA degrees, repeatedly heard faculty, and to a lesser extent staff, refer to the institution as the "Harvard of the Southeast." This is a campus of approximately 1000 students; the institution is focused on teaching, and they transfer their students to nearby four-year, regional comprehensives.

> CONSIDER:
>
> What do you suppose is the underlying meaning of this reference? Does this belief fit with mission? How might it provide a clue to Dean Outsider about the values of the campus? What, if anything, might Dean Outsider do with these insights?
>
> What genders and ethnicities did you imagine about these characters? (How) do any of your answers change based on their intersectional genders and ethnicities, in relation to other characters?

2. THE CASE OF THE DICKENSIAN DEPARTMENTS

Early in their tenure, Provost Earnest would repeatedly hear snarky comments regarding the colossal size of the budget in the office of the provost at any meeting where resource allocation was mentioned. Dr. Dogma would make long, impassioned statements at senate meetings railing against the heinous imbalance of funding, likening academic departments to the impoverished characters in a Dickens novel. Dogma was praised and admired by faculty colleagues for having the courage to speak truth to power.

Knowing that the statements about the budget were not true, Earnest decides to email the entire academic affairs budget with spending details, to every person working in the division. This unexpected move resulted in shock and anger among the faculty. In reality, the provost's office had only 10% of the academic affairs budget and some of the largest budgets were in departments with the fewest students (including Dr. Dogma's department). Once the myth was dispelled, a major plank was removed from Dr. Dogma's platform as the self-appointed moral center of the campus, and they did not speak during the remaining senate meetings for the semester.

After the public release of the budget, Provost Earnest developed a new budget model that more closely aligned with enrollment in each department, and there was very little pushback. The only people who openly complained were faculty in units where the budgets were disproportionately large compared to the number of students they served—an inequity enabled by the lack of transparency and the acceptance of rumor as truth. In the end, a few people stepped down from the moral high ground and humbly but privately apologized to the provost, admitting that they had never asked for nor seen any budget figures, but had blindly accepted and spread the rumor.

> CONSIDER:
>
> What purpose(s) did the budget myth serve? Why would faculty not request to see the budget given the rumor of the gross funding imbalance?

Unexpectedly releasing the budget was a guerilla tactic. Given that the rumor was widely accepted, was this the best or only way the provost could squash it? What other actions might the provost have taken to share the truth about the budget?

What genders and ethnicities did you imagine about these characters? (How) do any of your answers change based on their intersectional genders and ethnicities, in relation to other characters?

SECTION TWO: POWER DYNAMICS

3. THE CASE OF THE INVISIBLE INEQUITIES

Andy Administrator serves on the policy committee of their campus. In response to a severe budget deficit over several years, HR is asking to change the policy related to the institutional contribution to retirement, lowering it from a 10% to a 5% match. The match has always been linked to a 2% contribution by the employee, which would stay the same. The change would take place as soon as the president approves it, pending committee recommendation. As the committee discusses it, they see it as applicable to all employees and therefore, unbiased. Andy realizes that a blanket policy of reduction will penalize those who are closer to retirement, and that the need for an employee match has been and will continue to be inequitable, since not all employees have 2% disposable income to invest.

CONSIDER:

How might Andy bring this up to the policy committee during deliberations? Should Andy mention this to the president, if the committee recommends the policy changes?

What genders and ethnicities did you imagine about these characters? (How) do any of your answers change based on their intersectional genders and ethnicities, in relation to other characters?

4. The Case of the Missing Hair Salons (It's Not Us, It's Them)

Alex Assistant is serving on a departmental search committee for a new hire. Alex notices that every time the committee considers a suspected or obvious BIPOC candidate, one or more other members of the committee will bring up the unwelcoming nature of the local community, and on more than one occasion, Alex has heard them say, "And there are no hair salons that cut Black people's hair."

CONSIDER:

What biases is Alex hearing?

How might Alex address this, assuming Alex identifies as white?

Section Two: Power Dynamics

How might Alex address this, assuming Alex identifies as a BIPOC?

To whom might Alex bring this up?

Are there any recommendations you might make as to the preparation for search committees, given these comments?

5. The Case of the Homespun Hires

Alex Assistant is again serving on a departmental search committee for a new hire. This time, Alex notices that the other committee members seem to mention 'good fit' when discussing candidates who are current adjuncts or those who earned degrees from either their program as an undergraduate or Master's student, or from the institution's doctorate in higher education leadership. They seem to always have reasons to exclude or provide a lower ranking for external candidates.

CONSIDER:

What biases is Alex hearing?

How might Alex address this, assuming Alex earned degrees outside the institution? To whom might Alex bring this up?

How might Alex address this, assuming Alex earned a degree from this institution? To whom might Alex bring this up?

Are there any recommendations you might make as to the preparation for search committees, given these comments?

What genders and ethnicities did you imagine about these characters? (How) do any of your answers change based on their intersectional genders and ethnicities, in relation to other characters?

2.3. Setting Boundaries

"No is a complete sentence." —Anne Lamott

> **KEY CONCEPTS AND CONSIDERATIONS**
>
> - Power dynamics exist, given hierarchies.
> - Everyone attends to these hierarchies, but in different ways.
> - You need to attend to them by setting boundaries.
> - Know your role.
> - Know the role of others.

In the last two sections, we briefly introduced *power dynamics* and *hierarchy*, specifically as these relate to your role in the organizational chart and to the campus climate regarding gender and ethnicity. Power dynamics means that some people have more control over others, whether by how roles are structured or by one's location regarding gender, ethnicity, sexual orientation, class status, and other characteristics. Others have written extensively about these topics—too many to list here. However, a good place to start to understand institutional power dynamics regarding race is the online bibliography link at the Racial Equity Institute.[3]

In your leadership role, it is useful to think about power embedded in the formal structure. Think of the person you report to. One way to think about power dynamics is to consider what you would say to your direct supervisor: Would you pick your words more carefully than if you were saying something similar to a friend? To someone who reports to you?

Now, take a moment to consider the list of your direct reports, and those who report to them, which means they indirectly report to you. They are probably careful about what they say to you and how they say it. They are aware of who has power, just as you are aware when you think of your own supervisor. Even if your style is egalitarian, power dynamics exist, and people under you notice this.

---

[3] The Racial Equity Institute's bibliography is available at www.racialequityinstitute.com/bibliography.

People will see you as your role, not as a person. When we were in various leadership roles—president, provost, dean, vice president—we thought of ourselves as "Susan" or "Maria," who happened to be *in* a role, as did our friends. However, people who know you in that role, even if you are promoted from within, will see you *as* the role. This does not leave much room for assuming best intentions when you make a mistake. They also will read motivations into your behavior in ways that may or may not be true.

Given these power dynamics, setting boundaries or limits is important from day one. Boundaries pertain to sharing information and assignment of tasks. Even sharing casual opinions can be fraught. Of course, people will know some things about you, whether you disclose those things or not, and will make 'meaning' about you based on what you do disclose. What meaning might people make if you talk about a vacation building homes for Habitat for Humanity, compared to a luxury cruise to Monte Carlo? What impression is created if you drive a new Mercedes SUV, compared to a small sedan that is an electric hybrid?

If you see yourself as just "you" in a role, you may want to share more of yourself. It's tempting. However, we have learned that it's important to keep firm boundaries from the beginning. Keep them firm longer than you think you need to. You can always loosen them, but it is very difficult to tighten them. Take the time to figure out who you can trust, such as those people who appear to be ethical across contexts, before you loosen boundaries. Even so, you will want to be careful to stretch them only with select people. Remember, you never have to loosen them if you don't want to.

If you want to figure out which boundaries to set and with whom, you can start with the organizational structure. Structure can include organizational charts and job description. Both can be useful, but they are limited. They don't tell you how effective someone is in performing their duties, nor do they let you know whether positions have the same level of access to information you have. However, once you see the structure, you can then try to determine the scope of your role and that of others. You will be able to determine who is a peer, a subordinate, or a supervisor.

For your direct reports, part of setting boundaries is to be consistent in your communication and limits. State your expectations of yourself and others, both explicitly and implicitly. You can use delegation to help people learn what is their role, and what is yours.

Later, as you settle into your role, you may wish to loosen boundaries. Perhaps you need others to know sensitive information. Sometimes, in order to build relationships, we want to share more about ourselves so that people get to know the person behind the role.

Before you can decide which boundaries, if any, to loosen, you need to know whom you can trust, and about what. People have to demonstrate that they have the ability to respect boundaries. Avoid messy people. Examples include people who are often involved in complaints (maybe not directly) and/or people who always need special accommodations.

How do you know if someone honors confidences? If they tell you things 'in confidence,' then they are likely to be telling others as well. Be mindful of the concept that *gossip/knowledge = power*, addressed in Section 2.2.

Section Two: Power Dynamics

If you think someone is trustworthy and you decide to loosen boundaries with them, test them with low-stakes information first. *Low stakes* means that the information can't do too much harm if they do share it with others. Or, in the spirit of maintaining clear boundaries, you could choose to *always* keep disclosures low stakes. For example, you might disclose to them your reports about budget projections prior to those being announced to the entire institution. We will cover more about whom to trust in Section Three.

Your social life can be impacted by your position of leadership. Whoever reports to or through you is probably not a good candidate for friendship, unless they have the exceptional ability to separate work and private life. It will be hard to leave power dynamics aside when socializing. If the institution is located in a larger city, you don't need to socialize outside of work roles. However, if your institution is located in a smaller community, you will need to decide about socializing with coworkers. The safe option is to only host gatherings centered on work (e.g., celebrate the start or end of the academic year) and invite all people from a specific work cohort.

If you want to become friends with someone at work, determine if the person can separate themselves and you from your work roles. You may need to accept that you may not be able to socialize normally, depending on your role and whether or not people on the campus can separate you from the power associated with your role. This may be a loss related to being in the leadership role.

It's a special case when you are promoted from within. Hopefully, friends won't see you as 'going to the dark side' when you take a leadership role. Yet you need to be prepared to accept that friendships may not survive your transition into the leadership role. Friends may not be able to adjust to seeing you in your new role or may not understand that you can't tell them everything. And you may see some less-than-flattering sides of people who have been your colleagues for years.

If you promote others from within—someone who is now a direct report to you—you may need to help them prepare for this transition. They may not have considered the possibility of their relationships changing due to power dynamics, nor will they know how to negotiate these changes. They need to be aware of this possibility before taking the new job. Once in their new position, you will need to be able to trust them with the appropriate duties and confidences, and they will need to set their own boundaries with former peers and friends.

Later in this section, you can explore these ideas further in four case studies:

- The Case of the Deputized Deans
- The Case of Mountains and Molehills
- The Case of the Open House That Became Too Hot to Handle
- The Case of the Research Hustle

MICROCONTEXT

1	Does the current organizational chart of your unit and/or the institution make sense to you, given other structures you have worked within? Is it piecemeal, or does it form a coherent whole? Does it even exist? Does it reflect the accurate function of your division/area?
2	Consider the location of your new institution geographically. Is it a big fish in a little pond, or vice versa?

SELF-REFLECTION

How comfortable are you with setting boundaries? Think of at least one example that went well and one that did not. What might you fear about setting boundaries?

What are the important initial boundaries in your current leadership position?

You may decide to never relax your boundaries. When might it be useful to relax them? What are the costs to *not* relaxing them? What are the risks if you do decide to relax them?

How do you know whom you can trust, and with what information can you trust them?

Section Two: Power Dynamics

What information might be useful to share (e.g., what boundaries can you loosen) initially, and a few months into the role?

What is your comfort level on socializing with colleagues?

If promoted from within, how might you navigate the shift? How will you set boundaries with former peers? How will it feel to be seen as joining the 'dark side?'

If you've ever moved up within an institution previously, what was helpful to you in navigating that transition and deciding how best to set boundaries at that time?

SECTION TWO: POWER DYNAMICS

ROADMAP 2.3

What is your plan for getting to know colleagues more socially within your role?

If you promote others from within, how will you help them learn how to set boundaries?

Case Studies

1. The Case of the Deputized Deans

Provost Earnest inherited a haphazard hiring process. Department chairs would ask deans for new or replacement positions year-round, and if either the chair or dean was in favor with the provost, they got the position. Replacement positions were considered a given and were promised to faculty by the deans. Previous provosts also interviewed all candidates and made the selection, based on scant input from the search committee and the deans. Provost Earnest decided that the process needed to be clarified and made more uniform, and as manager of the Academic Affairs personnel budget, the provost needed to be the 'decider' on which positions were allocated, as well as salary caps. The provost implemented an annual cycle of requests, with money freed up from the previous year's vacancies. Assignment of positions involved an inclusive process, which flowed from department chairs to each dean, who would rank the requests in their College. Collectively, the team of deans and provost would create a tentative list of funded positions, with the ultimate authority resting with the provost. Deans were then delegated to be in charge of the hiring process and became the 'deciders' for each new hire.

> CONSIDER:
>
> How did the process inherited by Provost Earnest muddy boundaries, and how did it misalign responsibility and authority?

Section Two: Power Dynamics

How were boundaries defined better by Provost Earnest? What communication was needed by Provost Earnest to help this process become clearer regarding the alignment of responsibilities and authority?

What genders and ethnicities did you imagine about these characters? (How) do any of your answers change based on their intersectional genders and ethnicities, in relation to other characters?

2. The Case of Mountains and Molehills

President Petry and Provost Earnest are rarely invited to attend the Faculty Senate meetings, making it difficult to advance important strategic directions for the institution. The executive committee of the Senate agrees to meet with them prior to and after each Senate meeting, with the stated purpose to discuss important strategic items. However, the president of the Faculty Senate, Abby Monkson, always starts the meeting with a list of minor concerns raised by the faculty, which then typically takes the whole meeting time. When questioned, Abby notes that these little items can get out of control very quickly, and the intent is to help solve them before they can grow. President Petry and Provost Earnest often and gently point out the purpose of the meeting, but to no avail. Abby continues to engage in hyperbolic agenda items, and they are often seen as a 'savior' by the faculty, who increasingly send them all of their concerns, no matter how small—even if the concern is noticed only by an n of 1.

CONSIDER:

(Where) are there boundary issues in this case study?

What else might President Petry and Provost Earnest do to advance strategic priorities within this meeting? What would it take to make that even possible?

Section Two: Power Dynamics

What genders and ethnicities did you imagine about these characters? (How) do any of your answers change based on their intersectional genders and ethnicities, in relation to other characters?

3. The Case of the Open House That Became Too Hot to Handle

Provost Earnest had been on the job for several months and decided that it was time to hold an informal social gathering of chairs, directors, deans, and their significant others at the provost's home, with their spouse hosting as well. The provost thought it was clear in their invitation that it was an 'open house,' meaning that folks might drop in between 3-6 p.m. one afternoon. Somehow, word spread that it was a housewarming, and everyone showed up with gifts. Provost Earnest was quite uncomfortable and never entertained colleagues in their home again. Multiple jars of homemade jam gifts still line the pantry shelves.

CONSIDER:

What power dynamics were at play regarding this invitation and during the event?

What could Provost Earnest have done differently ahead of the event, or after it became an unintended housewarming, complete with gifts?

Section Two: Power Dynamics

Was the choice to never hold another event in the home a good idea?

What genders and ethnicities did you imagine about these characters? (How) do any of your answers change based on their intersectional genders and ethnicities, in relation to other characters?

4. The Case of the Research Hustle

Harper Hustle was one of the most respected faculty researchers on campus and was also well-liked, having a friendly and generous nature. Tanner True, newly appointed to the role of Associate Provost, learned through one of the duties of their position that Harper had plagiarized on their CV, claiming to have published some research that didn't exist or that wasn't theirs. Up until now, they had mutual friends and had socialized together on numerous occasions. Tanner isn't comfortable socializing with Harper anymore and stops attending mutual gatherings. Friends ask Tanner why they are no longer hanging out, and they are evasive, which has an impact on those friendships as well. Tanner didn't realize that the promotion might have these types of implications.

CONSIDER:

Were there other options for Tanner, and if so, what might those options be?

How could Tanner have been better prepared for the losses that result from internal promotion? Who might have helped Tanner prepare for this type of situation?

Section Two: Power Dynamics

What genders and ethnicities did you imagine about these characters? (How) do any of your answers change based on their intersectional genders and ethnicities, in relation to other characters?

SECTION THREE: RELATIONSHIP BUILDING

1. Building Internal and External Relationships: Identifying the Important Stakeholders
2. Information Gathering and Determining Who to Trust (and About What)
3. Examining Shared Governance (Generally)

If you take away the stately buildings and landscaped grounds, colleges and universities are people. Some of these people are central to the daily functioning of higher education, such as the students, staff, faculty, administrators, alumni, and trustees. Others are in the institution's orbit, such as employers, students' families, and politicians.

In Section Three, you will be immersed in the *who* and the *how* of building good relationships to support your goals. Building on Section Two, this section will also provide guidance on how to build multi-directional trust within the power-laden dynamics of the institution. Lastly, this section will aid you, as a leader, in developing strategies for the successful use of shared governance.

3.1. Building Internal and External Relationships: Identifying the Important Stakeholders

> **KEY CONCEPTS AND CONSIDERATIONS**
>
> - Identify key stakeholders almost immediately, both inside and outside the institution.
>
> - Know and acknowledge the perspective(s) of all stakeholder groups.
>
> - Develop relationships with stakeholders *before* a crisis, not after or because of one.
>
> - Understand the importance of people to getting things done.

In order to get most tasks accomplished in higher education, we must rely on people, either via delegation or via collaboration. Relationship building, therefore, is a key task. And the relationships built can be the difference between success, stagnation, or failure. You will need to identify key stakeholders almost immediately, both inside and outside the institution. It is also best if you can develop relationships during a calm period, when there is no crisis. Having to get to know people *in* a crisis can make the situation even more difficult to manage.

Who are the people inside your institution, with whom you need to develop relationships? There are both formal and informal ways to figure this out. Formally, you can use organizational charts. While these can provide some idea of the scope of others' jobs and where they align within the institution, there are limitations. For example, organizational charts can hide who is good at what tasks, what relationships exist informally between others, and the further meanings behind the organizational chart.

You will also want to form relationships with the opinion leaders at the institution, and there is no formal way to uncover these people. They are often not readily visible, and others on campus will not tell you directly who they are. They are typically people who have earned respect on campus by their longevity, or by speaking or performing in ways that are congruent with what is valued at the institution. For example, at one campus, there was a faculty member who was held in great esteem by others because he had an international reputation as a scholar. However, he did no service and therefore had limited direct knowledge of institutional data or processes. Yet this did not stop others from listening to his opinions about everything at the Faculty Senate.

The Work of Building Relationships

The purpose of developing relationships is to be able to work together effectively, not to be best friends. You can develop relationships via regular workflow/tasks or with more intentionality.

YOUR DIRECT REPORTS AND PEERS

Some of the best relationships can be built over a shared task. Perhaps counterintuitively, stronger relationships can be forged when the task at hand presents some difficulties to overcome together as a group.

Sometimes, there are no shared tasks. Or you will need to get to know others before those opportunities arise. You can decide if you want to meet one on one, or in groups, to get to know people. How you decide to develop working, collegial relationships may vary based on whether you are an introvert or an extrovert. Introverts are better one on one, or in small groups discussing ideas. Extroverts may want larger-group social interactions.

Do not underestimate the importance of routine recognition, such as special notes regarding accomplishments (such as publications). Sending a congratulatory note to people doesn't take much time but is noticed and often appreciated. Also, we once heard someone describe "the long walk back from lunch"; they would often stroll down different hallways and just chat with others they ran into. There was no agenda, no pressure, just a friendly way to meet people. The long walk also served to help develop relationships outside of a crisis situation. However, with intense schedules, that long walk is often just not possible.

YOUR SUPERVISOR

Sometimes, you are building a relationship with your supervisor. One part of this is the formal, supervisory process. Another part of this specific relationship involves 'managing up'—that is, how to keep them informed at the right level of detail within their role. In general, do not surprise them. Keep them informed of anything that might be problematic, even if not probable. Also, even if it is difficult, you should have their back. Do not bad-mouth them to others at the institution, no matter how tempted. You can expect that they will take credit for what you do, much as their own supervisor will take credit for their work, too.

If you have a formal role with anyone higher up the reporting structure (above your supervisor), use discretion. Whether they are a VP or the president or on the Board of Trustees, don't tell them anything that you haven't already shared with your supervisor.

YOUR EXTERNAL COMMUNITY

So far, we have discussed building relationships within your institution. There are important relationships to be built outside the institution as well. Are you part of a state system or are you private/independent? If a private institution, you may need or want to find a peer group. One of us started a peer group in the region that met two to three times a year. It was great to share ideas about areas of common interest and concerns.

The size of a community may impact opportunities to build external relationships, and with whom. If you live in a smaller community—one in which the institution is a large employer—you may need to manage overlapping relationships. For example, in smaller communities, you may be the neighbor of a member of the Board of Trustees, or those who report to you may be related to the owner of a local business you frequent.

To connect to others in the community, you can join the 'Leadership X' process often sponsored by the Chamber of Commerce. You may also provide service on local agency boards; this is an important way to meet people and understand local climate/culture.

If your institution is part of a state system, the system office may or may not encourage constituency groups meeting together. Determine just who your peers in the system are, and how you want/need to connect with them. Consider what you might learn from their experiences. Keep in mind the system's culture of transparency or competition, and determine if your peers in the state system are comfortable sharing information or if the culture is too competitive. You can then determine if you want to spend time with them, and if so, toward what ends.

There is a group of people who have roles both inside and outside the institution: alumni. Alumni have a lot of influence, and many employees at an institution can be alumni. For example, what if someone you supervise needs an annual review, but is a donor to the institution? Sometimes, politically, it will be difficult to give negative feedback if that employee gives substantial amounts to the institution. (This is another example of how overlapping relationships can be tricky to manage.) Also, developing relationships with alumni can be tricky if you are not an alumnus yourself. You may need to prove yourself if you are an outsider; by contrast, if you are an alumnus, you may get undeserved credit.

Lastly, you will find yourself in a double bind as you build internal and external relationships. Expectations in your role will vary; each type of relationship will bring a different idea of what you should be doing in your role. Your supervisor will have one set of expectations for you, based on both written and unspoken job duties. Your direct reports will have yet another set of expectations; students will have still another, and community members will have yet something else again. You can't control their expectations; just be aware that they will vary and that you would do well to use your own expectations and values to guide your behavior.

Later in this section, you can explore these ideas further in four case studies:

- The Case of the Manufactured Marriage
- The Case of the Introverted Interim
- The Case of the Dense Dean
- The Case of the Alumni Insiders

MICROCONTEXT

1	Review the organizational charts you reflected on in item 1 of the *Microcontext* in Section 2.3, page 94. Were any units created due to reasons other than functional proximities?

2 | List current organizational groups (e.g. cabinet? councils?) and how often they meet:

Group *Frequency of meeting*

_____ _____

_____ _____

_____ _____

_____ _____

_____ _____

3 | Is your institution part of a state higher education system or independent? Are there peers who hold similar roles to yours within the system or at nearby campuses with whom you can connect?

Section Three: Relationship Building

4	How do you want/need to connect with those peers? What might you learn from their experiences?
5	What is the culture of transparency or competition? Are peers within a state system or at nearby institutions comfortable sharing information, or are peers competitive in ways that affect achieving your goals?
6	What size of community do you live in? How large a 'fish' is your institution in that pond?

7 | Thinking about your institution's Board of Trustees:

- Are they clear about their role?

- Do they get too involved operationally—or are they not engaged enough?

- How political is their appointment?

- How able are they to critically examine the performance of the president?

Section Three: Relationship Building

8 | What dual relationships already exist within the institution and/or your unit?

9 | How large of an employee/alum cohort is there at your institution? How do they use their voice?

SELF-REFLECTION

Are you an introvert or an extrovert? How does this aspect of your personality impact your ability or willingness to build new relationships for your work? What are the pros and cons related to being an introvert or extrovert when building relationships?

SECTION THREE: RELATIONSHIP BUILDING

ROADMAP 3.1

List the important internal and external stakeholders in your current leadership position:

Who do you need to develop a relationship with horizontally?

Who do you need to develop a relationship with vertically?

List the meetings you need to conduct and how frequently.

Meeting   *Frequency*

_____   _____

_____   _____

_____   _____

_____   _____

_____   _____

_____   _____

_____   _____

_____   _____

_____   _____

How do you want to modify the current meetings to make them useful (and kept to a minimum)?

Section Three: Relationship Building

Think of quick and easy ways to build relationships via recognition:

Given the position of your institution in the community, what types of service do you need to do?

Are there local/state leadership boards you want to join (e.g., Chamber, Leadership County/State/City, etc.)?

How might you connect with your peers through existing structures (or set one up)?

Case Studies

1. THE CASE OF THE MANUFACTURED MARRIAGE

President Petry is trying to understand the organization that they have inherited and is starting with organizational charts. Interestingly, the institution has a VP over Student Success, who oversees both the traditional student affairs areas and Advancement/Foundation. As Petry explores further, they discover that this merger occurred when the former VP for student success retired during a time of budget shortfalls. Petry isn't sure this is an effective structure to support the institution's goals.

> CONSIDER:
>
> What variables might President Petry consider as they determine whether to continue the organizational structure as-is or change it? What are the pros and cons of all options?

What genders and ethnicities did you imagine about these characters? (How) do any of your answers change based on their intersectional genders and ethnicities, in relation to other characters?

SECTION THREE: RELATIONSHIP BUILDING

2. THE CASE OF THE INTROVERTED INTERIM

The university's chief advancement officer is taking family leave for six weeks to care for an aging parent who is seriously ill. The associate VP, who would ordinarily step in to lead the unit, recently accepted a promotion at another institution, and their departure was followed by two other people in key positions leaving the institution. Due to these vacancies, the director for advancement analytics, Remmy Reserved, is now the most senior person in the office and must take on the role of chief advancement officer for six weeks. Remmy is an introvert whose comfort level does not go beyond working alone crunching numbers, generating reports, and wearing Star Trek t-shirts in the back office. Remmy dreads having to get dressed up to face a calendar full of fundraising events and attend football games in the president's suite with Big Bucks Bentley and other major donors or potential major donors.

CONSIDER:

A conscientious employee, Remmy wants to do a good job but is not sure how to approach the situation. Suggest ways Remmy can successfully fulfill the interim assignment.

What genders and ethnicities did you imagine about these characters? (How) do any of your answers change based on their intersectional genders and ethnicities, in relation to other characters?

3. THE CASE OF THE DENSE DEAN

Dean Lackey was charged with overseeing the selection of a department chair, of a department which is already fractured along gender lines. The departmental bylaws require each candidate to present to the other faculty, followed by an anonymous vote, which is shared in the aggregate with all faculty. Since there are two candidates for this election, Dean Lackey inserts a requirement for the vote: each voting member must first vote acceptable/nonacceptable for each candidate, followed by a ranking of the acceptable candidates. The following occurs:

- Candidate One, who is male, is voted in as chair, with unanimous acceptable votes.
- Candidate Two, who is female, receives several nonacceptable votes.

Provost Earnest finds out about this when Candidate Two tells President Petry about this, hinting at a lawsuit.

CONSIDER:

How might the surprise to both supervisor(s) and the outcome have been averted? How might Provost Earnest and/or President Petry deal with this, and with whom?

What genders and ethnicities did you imagine about these characters? (How) do any of your answers change based on their intersectional genders and ethnicities, in relation to other characters?

4. The Case of the Alumni Insiders

President Petry reviews the annual summary of university data. A data point that stands out is the large percentage of employees who are also alums. The president meets with Mona Volador, the HR director, and with a small group of alum employees to learn more about their needs. The participants suggest that a group be established to meet their special needs. The president tasks Mona with establishing the group.

CONSIDER:

What are some potential topics that can be covered in their meetings?

What genders and ethnicities did you imagine about these characters? (How) do any of your answers change based on their intersectional genders and ethnicities, in relation to other characters?

3.2. Information Gathering and Determining Who to Trust (and About What)

> *"Trust but verify."* —Ronald Reagan

> KEY CONCEPTS AND CONSIDERATIONS
>
> - Use multiple methods to determine who to trust.
> - Learn people's agendas.

Information Gathering

Data is necessary to effective leadership; once you are able to analyze data, you will be able to formulate the information you need to make decisions. You can think of *data* as the (mostly) objective, unfiltered input, while *information* is what is available to you after an analysis. Data is more often thought of as quantitative; however, qualitative data is also very useful, and can be gathered from others via more informal methods. As you consider gathering qualitative data, it is critical to look at the relationships in your leadership position and consider: How do you know whom to trust—and about what?

Let's explore *trust* in general a bit further before we elaborate on *data*. We will explore data in more detail at the end of this section.

Trust

People often think of trust as monolithic: you either trust someone, or you don't. However, trust is more complex than that. Whether or not to trust someone varies depending on context. You may trust your best friend with your most intimate thoughts, but if they are a bad driver, you may insist on driving when you go places together via car.

At its simplest, trust suggests reliability, congruency, and honesty over time, and is demonstrated through behavior.

SECTION THREE: RELATIONSHIP BUILDING

Trust is typically built over time. However, those same behaviors that build trust slowly and with repetition can, when observed in a highly charged, high-stakes situation, create trust almost immediately.

Typically, trust is mutual. It is hard to trust others if they don't trust you (about the salient context). That is, there may be someone that you trust to do their job duties well, but you suspect they bad-mouth you behind your back. This would impact the ability to have a truly authentic, trusting relationship overall.

Trust is not about agreement, either. It's about the possibility and commitment to work through conflicts or disagreements authentically and respectfully. Power dynamics can make it difficult to have authentic trust between people.

Let's examine different types of relationships and how approaches to trust may vary. Note that there is only so much you can control when it comes to creating trust in you. For all of the following suggestions, congruency is of the utmost importance.

Your Direct Reports and Peers

Let's start with how to create trust in you by those you supervise. You can set clear expectations for your direct reports and those who report through you. If you change these expectations, be clear about when and how they change. For example, you may have made a decision that you later need to change. If you must change the direction regarding something of importance, be honest. Provide as much context as possible and provide the reason for your change of mind. Try not to make any promises unless you can absolutely keep them. Sometimes, there are situations in which you make a commitment in good faith, but have the decision overturned by your supervisor. Try to get support from your supervisor before publicly making commitments to important decisions.

Often, people who report to you will conflate trust and transparency. They will claim lack of transparency when they don't know all the facts and details, which can be true. Unfortunately, leaders often have information that they can't share—due to personnel confidentiality, for example. And some leaders just aren't transparent. However, people may sometimes claim lack of transparency even when the decision was made with as much transparency as possible. For example, people may make this claim when they don't agree with the decision, or if they think they should have more input in the decision itself. To garner trust, gather data/information from the people most impacted by the issue at hand. Be clear about whose decision it is. If it is yours to make, be clear about that fact and own it. Provide enough details, to the fullest extent possible, to frame the decision you make. These same guidelines will help you to build trust with your peers as well.

Your Supervisor

You will also want to build mutual trust and a shared understanding with your supervisor. The same suggestions made immediately above, for creating trust with your direct reports and peers, also apply here. Meet with your supervisor early and often. Find the right level of detail to share with them, to ensure that they are not surprised.

Be congruent over time, and be sure your words match your actions, both in private meetings with them and in larger group meetings. Do not criticize them to anyone at work. Admit any mistakes you make.

TRUST AMONG YOUR TEAM

Lastly, you will want your team of direct reports to build trust among themselves. This will enhance their ability to work effectively as a team and advance the initiatives of your unit. To facilitate this, you might share some of the ideas about trust in this section with your team and discuss.

Learn People's Agendas

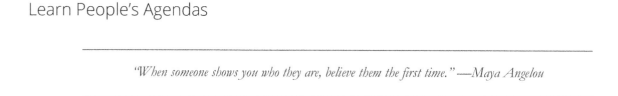

"When someone shows you who they are, believe them the first time." —Maya Angelou

Whether or not you can trust someone, you may still need to work with them. Learning who they are and what motivates them is important. At best, learning others' agendas may lead to truly productive working relationships, based on trust; at worst, it will at least help you to know who you are working with; this will increase the chance of a productive, albeit not so trusting or respectful, working relationship.

Maya Angelou said, "When someone shows you who they are, believe them." Keep your eyes and ears open in those first few meetings with people. If you are new to both the institution and the role, you may notice that your schedule fills up almost immediately with people who want to meet you. We have found that many people will almost immediately seek out those in new leadership roles. They will tell you stories—about themselves and about others. Sometimes they will tell you what they need directly, and other times, they are laying the groundwork for asking you at a later time. What they choose to tell you is the history that they think is important. Pay attention to who is the first in the door, and to what they say or don't say. All of this is good information about what their agenda is and their style in achieving it. They are showing you who they are. Believe them.

Remember Section 2, on power dynamics and politics? Keep these dynamics in mind when hearing people's introductory stories. While they are telling you who they are, they are also trying to figure out who *you* are as a supervisor or a peer. Monitor your reaction to their stories. This is not the time to wholeheartedly agree or disagree, but rather a time to listen and reflect.

The history and the stories they tell offer you the opportunity to ask questions to fill in information they might be omitting. You might also be able to draw some preliminary observations about the culture of the institution. When one of us started at a new institution, almost every person's introductory meetings included stories with comments about who was to blame for past failures. They quickly learned that part of the agenda of many at the institution was to assign blame to someone else before they themselves could be held accountable.

If you are new at an institution, you will not have the history of past interactions to inform your impressions of people. What you will have is their current behavior and what they tell you about their past behavior. *They are showing you who they are. Believe them.* We repeat this because it can be hard to do. And it's so important to remember, because the best predictor of future behavior is past behavior.

Ways to Gather Data

In Section 3.1, we focused on the informal, qualitative ways to gather data and create information to inform your working relationships. You can also utilize quantitative data to help understand the overall context of what is working well and what needs improvement.

IR

Each institution should have a formal institutional research (IR) function. Unit titles may vary, as does how the data is used. Typically, reports developed by these units are the official and most accurate data. They will, however, include the assumptions made in compiling the reports. If available, you can use official dashboards to see how well units are doing in contributing to strategic goals and directions. If such dashboards don't exist, these may be something you will want to create. When one of us was president, one of their first acts was to create a transparent data dashboard, aligned with measurable strategic directions. This dashboard was updated daily and was visible to everyone at the campus. This transparency was not always embraced, but it did allow for all those in leadership to see both their performance as well as the performance of others. This helped to create an institutional framework from which to work together.

UNIT REPORTS

Unit reports are another source of both formal and informal data. The formal data includes the content covered, such as past and future goals set and their measurements of achievement. Informal data might include how well the report is written, and how the successes and failures are discussed.

All these sources of formal data provide a shorthand of how well the institution and/or units are doing. With care, you can extrapolate what this might mean about the people leading those units. For example, if a unit never reaches their modest goals, and the annual reports remain similar from year to year, this might suggest poor leadership in that unit, and that is something you might want to investigate further.

SHADOW SYSTEMS

Along with the official institutional data, most campuses will also have unit-level produced data, sometimes referred to as shadow systems. These often do not match the official data, and often are used to help support the needs of the unit. Sometimes the discrepancies are due to differing assumptions or to the date at which the data were produced. It is important that each institution has clear policies about what is official data, how and when it is used, and who holds the official data. As you build relationships and use data to inform them, be ready when provided with alternative sets of data. At most institutions, the most trustworthy data is the official data.

Later in this section, you can explore these ideas further in seven case studies:

- The Case of the Adjusted Agreement
- The Case of the Klingon High Council
- The Case of More Molehills
- The Case of the Chummy Buddies
- The Case of the Divergent Deans
- The Case of the Runaway Rumor
- The Case of the Finicky Faculty

MICROCONTEXT

1	Does your campus have an institutional research (IR) office? ___ Yes ___ No If yes, do you have access to their reports to use as a source of formal, quantitative information that shows past performance?
2	Do the staff in the institutional research office know how to conduct analysis, or do they just do nominal reporting?

Section Three: Relationship Building

3	To whom do they report?
4	Do they understand your role and your need to access data?
5	Who owns the official institutional data?
6	Are there programs to generate the reports you want?

| 7 | Do individual offices keep their own data? If so, how do they use their data? *Can* and/or *do* they articulate the assumptions? |

Qualitative data to consider...

| 8 | Who among the leadership team, staff, and/or faculty have the institution's common good in mind? |

| 9 | Who acts professionally? |

Section Three: Relationship Building

| 10 | Who has longevity and is still engaged and productive per their time at rank and role? |

| 11 | How transparent is the campus at all levels (e.g., do chairs/directors/VPs share ideas, data, and/or programs with others)? |

| 12 | What reports are available? Which reports are used most often? Which are not used? |

SELF-REFLECTION
Have you ever trusted someone who betrayed that trust?
Think of someone you trust now. How do you know you can trust them? And about what?

Section Three: Relationship Building

ROADMAP 3.2

First:

√ Make a list of the reports you need and get access to them.

√ Identify reports you need that are not generated. Working with the IR Office, develop these reports.

Then:

Decide how you want to use these reports, both existing and requested. Who do they need to be shared with, how, and when?

Case Studies

1. THE CASE OF THE ADJUSTED AGREEMENT

Based on the budget provided by the CFO, Provost Earnest has allocated positions for searches for the year. Dean Lackey is delighted to be awarded three positions, and quickly notifies the selected departments of the good news. A week later, Provost Earnest is told by the CFO that they had made a miscalculation, and that only two positions are possible for the next year in Dean Lackey's College; therefore, the third ranked position will not be possible. Provost Earnest has worked hard to build the trust of Dean Lackey and the faculty in that College.

> CONSIDER:
>
> What should Provost Earnest say to Dean Lackey? Should Provost Earnest disclose the mistake made by the CFO or provide any rationale? Should Provost Earnest communicate directly with the department that lost the position—or leave that messaging to Dean Lackey?
>
> What genders and ethnicities did you imagine about these characters? (How) do any of your answers change based on their intersectional genders and ethnicities, in relation to other characters?

SECTION THREE: RELATIONSHIP BUILDING

2. THE CASE OF THE KLINGON HIGH COUNCIL

The issue of transparency and trust is a recurring theme in President Petry's meetings with the Faculty Senate executive board. Feeling a need to make a good-faith effort to foster transparency and trust, the president establishes the position of Chief Data Officer (CDO). The president has observed the hard work and dedication of Remmy Reserved, the director for advancement analytics, who has just completed a six-week stint as interim chief advancement officer. The president offers the position to Remmy and the offer is accepted even before the president can finish the sentence.

Remmy is relieved to be in a role that will not require attendance at fundraising events. Responsible for crunching numbers and working behind the scenes again, Remmy is happy to return to wearing Star Trek t-shirts and staying out of the public eye. An added perk in the role of CDO is an office large enough to display models of Star Trek starships, including the Enterprise-D, a Klingon Bird of Prey, and a Romulan T'Met with Tal Shiar emblem, all revolving around several M-class planets.

Remmy knows that the university has a large cache of data assets but realizes that the consistent use of data is limited to a few people and a few units. To remedy this, Remmy proposes a data democratization project to provide live data, in the aggregate, to all employees. Remmy receives the president's blessing and gets to work. The project opens up the president's executive dashboard, which is updated every night at 11:00 p.m., to every single employee. The dashboard includes data from every academic department and each division-level unit. The president asks Remmy to present and explain the dashboard at a special joint meeting of the cabinet and the Faculty Senate executive board. Remmy is honored and excited to be asked to present to the university's version of the Klingon High Council.

During the presentation, Remmy notices that everyone is silent and pensive, and they open the floor for questions at the end. Abby Monkson, president of the Faculty Senate, is the first to speak. "Am I to understand that this dashboard displays data from every academic program for the whole campus to see?"

Remmy confirms this.

Abby speaks again. "When I talked about transparency, I only thought about sharing data to see what administrators are doing. It never occurred to me that data from every academic program would be shared."

Remmy reminds Abby that the data on the dashboard is all public information, and now it's just easier to access.

A few people in the room—faculty and cabinet members—are pleased, as they have often asked colleagues for information but have never received it. Others are feeling "exposed" and are not sure they want their colleagues in other departments to see their academic programs' less than stellar student retention and graduation rates. One department chair is visibly upset that others can see that their department's enrollment represents less than 1% of total enrollment. The chief advancement officer hopes no one notices that they missed their target for alumni giving in Quarter 1. The president adjourns the meeting, and an animated discussion continues in the hallway as several people give Remmy the stink eye. A confused and frustrated Remmy mumbles a few curse words in Klingon and returns to the office to work on other projects.

CONSIDER:

What kind of advance work could have taken place to prepare people for the presentation and to lessen the feeling of exposure? How can the dashboard be used to promote trust?

What genders and ethnicities did you imagine about these characters? (How) do any of your answers change based on their intersectional genders and ethnicities, in relation to other characters?

3. The Case of the Finicky Faculty

Dean Outsider wants to help department chairs learn to use data to support their decisions and requests. In one attempt, Dean Outsider provides each department with the number of students enrolled in their department per major. Dean Outsider is immediately met with a chorus of questions and accusations by every department about the inaccuracy of the numbers. Dean Outsider was quite clear when sharing the data that it was based on the official IPEDS report. This data is frozen on the 10th day of enrollment, and does not count any double students who have double majors.

> CONSIDER:
>
> Are there any other assumptions that Dean Outsider might have provided?
>
>
>
> Is the data valid to use to make decisions?

How might Dean Outsider work with department chairs to use this data?

What genders and ethnicities did you imagine about these characters? (How) do any of your answers change based on their intersectional genders and ethnicities, in relation to other characters?

SECTION THREE: RELATIONSHIP BUILDING

4. THE CASE OF MORE MOLEHILLS

Abby Monkson, Faculty Senate Chair, emails President Petry on Friday afternoon, stating that they must speak to the President about an urgent matter. This is not unusual; it happens about once a month. It seems that a faculty member has heard a rumor that their department will be closed. Abby tells the President that they mentioned the possibility in passing at a Senate meeting, but only as an example. This faculty member was not at the meeting but heard it from a colleague. Abby wants to meet immediately with the President—before the weekend—to clarify and discuss so that the President knows Abby is going to stop the rumor.

CONSIDER:

Since this happens at least once a month, should the President clear their schedule to meet with Abby that afternoon? Is there anything the President can do to stop Abby's pattern?

What genders and ethnicities did you imagine about these characters? (How) do any of your answers change based on their intersectional genders and ethnicities, in relation to other characters?

---

5. The Case of the Chummy Buddies

During a performance review, Dean Lackey mentioned to Provost Earnest that their leadership style is to be friendly with their department chairs. They believe that building this type of relationship lays a good foundation for later requests that might be conflictual. Earlier in the year, Provost Earnest asked Dean Lackey to make a possibly difficult request—to ask Department Chair Pat Pompous to lead the department through significant curricular revisions. Months later, Provost Earnest checks in with Dean Lackey about the status of those revisions. Dean Lackey confesses that nothing has been done—much to their surprise, since Dean Lackey asked Pat to do it months ago.

CONSIDER:

Should Provost Earnest be surprised at these results? What patterns of behavior might have predicted this lack of action?

What genders and ethnicities did you imagine about these characters? (How) do any of your answers change based on their intersectional genders and ethnicities, in relation to other characters?

SECTION THREE: RELATIONSHIP BUILDING

6. THE CASE OF THE DIVERGENT DEANS

Provost Earnest is working with all the deans to allocate funds for academic equipment. Dean Lackey, in a demanding tone, states that all their requests must be honored; every one of them is necessary and of equal value, and they just can't provide a rank order. Dean Outsider provides a ranking of their requests, and states that while they would like all of these to be funded, their ranking provides the provost with input about what is really needed this year. Other requests, Dean Outsider notes, can wait until next year or might be funded via other institutional accounts or external funding possibilities, or are not really needed but are requested by chairs nonetheless.

CONSIDER:

Which of the deans' requests might carry more weight with Provost Earnest? What is it about that request that builds credibility with Provost Earnest? Does that credibility apply only to this process or might it generalize?

What genders and ethnicities did you imagine about these characters? (How) do any of your answers change based on their intersectional genders and ethnicities, in relation to other characters?

7. THE CASE OF THE RUNAWAY RUMOR

Sydney Suckup, a very ambitious director, follows President Petry out of the dining hall to make small talk and heap lashings of compliments on the president on a near-daily basis. The president is courteous, but curious as to why Sydney does this. It all seems harmless, so the president continues the chats. One day, Sydney reveals a desire to eventually ascend to the presidency and asks the president to be a mentor. Put on the spot but not wanting to upset Sydney, the president gives a vague answer that Sydney decides to interpret as a yes.

Sydney runs back to the office break room after lunch to tell everyone that the president is grooming them to be the university's next president. Sydney's officemates find the story somewhat believable given the numerous times Sydney and the president have been seen walking out of the dining hall together. Word spreads throughout the campus until it reaches the president. Even a couple of cabinet members and a board member, Big Bucks Bentley, ask if there is any truth to the rumor. The rumor begins to take on a life of its own as it is passed from person to person, negatively impacting the president's relationship with key stakeholders on campus. President Petry is not happy and realizes that the seemingly harmless small talk with Sydney has created this situation.

> CONSIDER:
>
> How should the president interact with Sydney in the future? How should the president respond when asked about the rumor? Should cabinet members, the board member, and other inquiring employees receive the same response from the president?

Section Three: Relationship Building

What genders and ethnicities did you imagine about these characters? (How) do any of your answers change based on their intersectional genders and ethnicities, in relation to other characters?

3.3. Examining Shared Governance

> *"A first step is to make sure that everyone understands that the sharing in 'shared governance' isn't equally distributed, nor does it imply decision-making authority. That authority is held by the president and the board, the ones who are accountable for both results and shortcomings."* —Scott S. Cowen

> **KEY CONCEPTS AND CONSIDERATIONS**
>
> - Shared governance is a term that is widely used and often misunderstood.
>
> - It's important that there is consensus on its meaning for each constituency on campus.
>
> - Look for efficiency in shared governance structures, since at its root is inefficiency.
>
> - Clarity about what shared governance is and isn't is essential for the productive functioning of the institution/unit.

Defining Shared Governance

Shared governance is a term that is widely used and often misunderstood. Shared governance defines various decision-making and consultative roles at a university, across students, faculty, staff, administrators, and the Board members. It can define both process and policy. Most businesses do not use this term, nor are they as explicit about these roles. If you come from a higher education background, you probably have some idea about what it means. However, if you are assuming a higher-education leadership role from outside the academy, you will want to make it a priority to learn more about shared governance.

Even if the term *shared governance* is used ubiquitously across higher education, each constituency at a university may define it differently. If constituents can reach a consensus about its meaning, this will greatly enhance the health of a university and its functioning. If no consensus exists—which is more often the norm than not—processes will be more difficult and may make progress almost impossible. In this case, the discussions will center on roles and rights to decision making, rather than on the issues themselves. Shared governance, at its root, is inefficient. A lack of shared definitions about how it operates at your institution will make it even more inefficient, perhaps obstructionist.

The good news is that a modified consensus *can* be reached and communicated. And it is possible for some shared governance structures, within a shared definition, to be both efficient and useful.

Given the importance of shared governance and of reaching a shared definition for it, it's important to start your new position with some knowledge of how it operates at your institution.

For faculty matters, you can start with a review of the Red Book of the AAUP. The Red Book clearly states that shared governance for faculty is tied to curriculum and rank and tenure processes. It also clearly states that the faculty role is consultative in other matters, and that decision making rests with administration. How consultation is defined and how it is used varies greatly from institution to institution. This may be the biggest source of misunderstanding on most campuses, as some people confuse consultation with decision-making authority. However, if a constituency can't be fired for the results of the decision, they are not the decision-making authority.

For faculty shared governance, committees elected by the faculty of the whole are typically the formal shared governance structures. For staff, if they have a Senate with membership of the whole, these Senates are the formal shared governance structures. Policies will often dictate other committees composed of elected members from these shared governance structures. For example, most campuses will have a budget committee, whose members include administrators (due to their positions), as well as faculty and staff membership who are elected by their constituent Senates or by an election of the whole. Which committees fall under this process will vary from campus to campus.

If you are new to an institution, be sure to determine which are the formal shared governance structures. You can review past climate/satisfaction surveys or minutes of shared governance committees at your institution to get some sense of actual practice and attitudes.

Shared governance is a separate concept from unions. However, if there are unions or a powerful AAUP chapter on a campus, this will significantly impact shared governance at the institution. At one institution where we worked, the Faculty Senate had a long history of being very productive and collaborative. However, a few years ago, a union officer was elected as Senate president. The Faculty Senate's business was conflated with union politics during that term, and never returned to the more collaborative model. If possible, determine how shared governance is impacted by the presence of unions at your institution.

Often, faculty and/or staff have the belief that shared governance is unidirectional; that is, they believe that shared governance means that their voices alone define shared governance. They forget that administrative roles are also part of the 'shared' concept. Also, they may or may not include students in the concept of shared governance.

If there is not a clear agreement on a definition of shared governance at the institution, you may wish to have your unit—or better yet, the entire campus—review all shared governance bodies and committees. You may need to use elected, shared governance representatives to create a task force to complete this work. If possible, consider how to use an external consultant to help facilitate the discussions, and someone who has a clear understanding of shared governance themselves. Be sure to implement a campus-wide communication to inform all parties about the purpose of the review and to ask for their participation and cooperation. To build consensus, you will need to use an iterative process in sharing and refining the definition. And, of course, share the final report with its recommendations with all stakeholders.

Defining Consultation

Consultation is another term that often needs to be specifically defined. Note whether there is a specific policy about this or if it is just an historically accepted practice. In the context of committees and/or task forces, write a clear charge, and be explicit that they are to make suggestions or recommendations, not binding decisions. Decision making is tied to consultation in shared governance. As mentioned above, if you can't be demoted or fired due to the salient decision, you are not the decision maker. People may need to be clear about *authority* vs. *responsibility/accountability*.

Consultation is valuable, in that it helps the decision maker to learn about various decisions that will have a potential impact on others. We believe that those who will be impacted more directly by the decision need to have input, and that their input needs to be afforded more weight than input from those not impacted directly. Often, even after consultation, people will be upset that their view did not prevail as the final decision. Within ethical and legal limits, share as much as you can about the rationale for decisions you make. This may help people to feel that their views were heard, even if their views did not ultimately result in driving the decision itself.

Reviewing Task Forces and Committees

When work needs to be done, you will be asked to use existing workgroups or to create new ones. Review the existing committees to see if their charge/role includes work to be done. If an appropriate shared governance structure already exists, use it. If none exist for a particular issue, and it's an area that impacts a lot of people, err on the side of creating shared governance task forces to get input. However, know that this will slow down any decisions made. Sometimes this is desired, if you do not want an idea to progress quickly. The inefficiency of shared governance processes can be both a blessing and a curse. In any case, its inefficiency is a reality to be considered in any timelines.

When you start your role, it's a good opportunity to clean house regarding committees. We advise you to review the existing committees to determine if they are still needed, and to eliminate some. Of the ones still needed, this may be an opportunity to refresh the committee's charge. Be sure to use the shared governance processes to undertake any eliminations or changes in the charges/purposes.

At one campus, we found committees that had not met in years, which we were able to eliminate. Some committees were combined. Everyone felt better that the committee structure had been made more streamlined. No one likes to do service that is not valuable. This streamlining also made personnel evaluations more meaningful, in that the supervisors/evaluators now knew that the committee work listed meant something, other than in name only.

We will discuss more specifics about the intersections of shared governance with various functions at an institution in Section Five.

Later in this section, you can explore these ideas further in four case studies:

- The Case of the Self-Assured Senators
- The Case of the Tire Tracks on the Back
- The Case of Mutiny in the Music Department
- The Case of the Center-Crazy Faculty

MICROCONTEXT

1	Determine: Do all constituency groups operate on the same definition of shared governance?
2	Where is there agreement and clarity across constituencies about shared governance roles at your current institution?

3	In what areas is there disagreement or lack of clarity about roles?
4	Who is included in shared governance on your campus?
5	What is the role of students in shared governance?
6	What is the role of staff in shared governance?

Section Three: Relationship Building

7. What is or is not considered consultation? Is this written in policy or is it an historically accepted practice?

8. Is it clearly understood who makes which decisions? Is this written in policy or is it an historically accepted practice?

9. Examine policies compared to organizational charts and practices. In what areas is the final decision maker the person who can be held accountable, and are there any areas in which these are disconnected?

10	Which bodies/committees are effective and contribute to the health of the institution/unit?
11	Which bodies/committees are moribund and need either to be re-established, reconfigured, repopulated, combined, or eliminated?
12	What is the role of the AAUP or unions on your campus, and how does this impact shared governance?

Section Three: Relationship Building

SELF-REFLECTION

Have there been times in your career when you used the inefficiency of shared governance to your advantage? Explain.

> **ROADMAP 3.3**
>
> √ Review the AAUP Red Book or faculty or staff contract and handbooks.
>
> √ Review past climate/satisfaction surveys or minutes of shared governance committees at your institution to get some sense of actual practice/attitudes.

Activity

The institution is facing a budget deficit next year but isn't sure just how much. President Petry is considering an across-the-board cut, but Provost Earnest knows that an across-the-board cut can hurt the institution. The provost delegates to you to figure out a more strategic approach. You decide, in the spirit of shared governance and in the importance of transparency, to form a university-wide task force to develop a recommendation-making process, resulting in three possible cuts: at 20%, 10%, or 5% deductions. The recommendation process should involve input from all constituencies.

Write a sample task force charge using the template provided on the next page.

GUIDELINES FOR WRITING A CHARGE

1. Write with clarity and parsimony.
2. Include an expectation of the use of data and what kind of data. Literature review? Quantitative/descriptive data?
3. Help them to locate data or provide it, if possible. From IR? Or do you expect them to gather it?
4. Note that they are expected to use data to inform recommendations.
5. Include expectations of the group, including a timeline and deliverable(s).

TEMPLATE FOR WRITING A CHARGE

Tip: Write with clarity and parsimony.

Context

Provide the background context as to the purpose and importance of the work to be done. Answer these questions: Why this work, and why now?

Composition of the Task Force

How many are to serve? From what areas of the institution? How are they to be selected/elected? To whom do they report? Who is the chair/facilitator, or do you ask them to select among themselves?

Deliverable(s)

What question(s) are they to answer, and how are their answers to be provided? (e.g., in a report of no more than XX pages—keep it brief; or in a presentation)

Data

Include your expectation for the use of data and what kind of data (e.g., literature review? quantitative/descriptive data?). Include information about where to find data. What are they expected to gather themselves? Who will provide them with data and what type? If possible, provide preliminary data with the charge.

Section Three: Relationship Building

Timeline

If possible, include a suggested timeline for tasks. Always include a deadline for completion.

Case Studies

1. THE CASE OF THE SELF-ASSURED SENATORS

In preparing for faculty and staff to return to campus in fall 2020 during COVID, the HR department has worked carefully with the campus health officer to follow the CDC guidelines. Included in those were criteria regarding employee behavior and safety protocols on campus, as well as criteria for waivers to work on campus. Led by Abby Monkson, the Faculty Senate sends a resolution to President Petry, insisting that they should review and decide on each waiver submitted by faculty; they make it clear that they think most, if not all, should be granted.

CONSIDER:

How does it fit, or not, within the purview of shared governance? Is any part of this a reasonable request within faculty shared governance? If so, what process/structure might be set up?

What genders and ethnicities did you imagine about these characters? (How) do any of your answers change based on their intersectional genders and ethnicities, in relation to other characters?

2. THE CASE OF THE TIRE TRACKS ON THE BACK

It's that time of year when Provost Earnest meets with all of the deans to get their input about allocation of faculty positions. This year, due to a substantial salary increase for all faculty, there is a very limited amount left in the personnel budget, only allowing for one new position. The provost and the deans discuss their Colleges' needs and the budget situation at length, over several meetings. Each dean is able to advocate strongly for their needs, and all come to consensus about the most compelling position needed: a position is allocated to a department in Dean Wink's College. Further, the deans discuss and strategize about how to communicate this news. At the next chairs' council, Dean Lackey tells their chairs that Provost Earnest just refused to allocate funding for any of their positions, offering no rationale. When meeting with the chairs in their college, Dean Outsider is told that this would never have happened under Dean Perfect.

CONSIDER:

Who is owning their responsibility and authority in this situation? What are the effects when blame is shifted to someone other than the person who oversees the unit? How/where are power dynamics operating in this case study?

What genders and ethnicities did you imagine about these characters? (How) do any of your answers change based on their intersectional genders and ethnicities, in relation to other characters?

3. The Case of Mutiny in the Music Department

The university's fall 2020 first-year class was down 7% from fall 2019, and returning students are down 5% due to the pandemic. Under ordinary circumstances, the university can make up any small downturns in fall enrollment the following spring by drawing on a large pool of community college transfers, but that will not happen this year. To make matters worse, fall 2021 enrollment projections do not look good. Provost Earnest and the deans are aware that they must begin planning for budget cuts and resource reallocation. The provost schedules a meeting with Abby Monkson, the Faculty Senate president, to clarify a consultation process.

Professor Singer, chair of the music department, is usually an advocate for using elected bodies to voice the faculty perspective. But in a lengthy email addressed to Provost Earnest and the dean, Professor Singer expresses distrust of even the music department's elected senators to properly represent the department in a senate full of people from larger departments with higher-demand programs. The email states that the stakes are too high to trust the Faculty Senate to advocate successfully for a very small and often overlooked department and that in times of economic downturn, the arts always seem to be the first thing to go. Therefore, states the professor, they will form their own separate consultation group that will meet with the provost and dean and that any feedback about the music department from the Faculty Senate should be disregarded. The chairs of several small departments get wind of mutiny in the music department and decide that they, too, will form their own independent groups.

CONSIDER:

How should Provost Earnest respond to Professor Singer and the other mutinous department chairs?

Section Three: Relationship Building

What genders and ethnicities did you imagine about these characters? (How) do any of your answers change based on their intersectional genders and ethnicities, in relation to other characters?

4. The Case of the Center-Crazy Faculty

The Board of Trustees, led by Big Bucks Bentley, has met with an ad hoc group of faculty to collaborate on increasing revenue, with a focus on increased grant writing. With dollar signs in their eyes, faculty were asked to submit proposals, and of the ten ideas submitted, eight of them focused on the creation of faculty-led Centers. The Centers ranged from providing summer camps to highly specialized research institutes. None of the proposals included how the Centers were to be funded, and all included significant workload reassignment for the Center director. Leading the charge, Abby Monkson asks the cabinet when these Centers can be formed. Provost Earnest and President Petry do not want these centers to be developed during these times of declining budgets.

CONSIDER:

How might Provost Earnest and President Petry use shared governance to explore these proposals or the establishment of Centers more generally?

What genders and ethnicities did you imagine about these characters? (How) do any of your answers change based on their intersectional genders and ethnicities, in relation to other characters?

SECTION FOUR: TEAM BUILDING

1. Team Building and Talent Acquisition
2. Skills and Competencies & Professional Development Needed
3. Matching Talent to Task Forces and Committees

Relationships get more complex when we meet and work in groups. Not only do teams need people with the content knowledge and expertise, they also need people who understand and engage in good communication skills and processes that embrace inclusion and collegiality. Teams include those who directly report to and through you, those engaged in ongoing committee work, and the more focused work of task forces.

Section Four explores how to create the teams you need in order to be successful—through an intentional approach to creating and influencing both their membership composition and effective processes. This section also explores how to develop capacity in future campus leaders through your intentional approach to team building.

4.1. Team Building and Talent Acquisition

"Look for competence, not claims." —Anthony de Mello

KEY CONCEPTS AND CONSIDERATIONS

- Assemble your team quickly. This requires a quick assessment of current talent to determine if there are gaps that you need to fill.

- Use multiple inputs to determine skills and competencies.

- Most work is done in teams.

Very little work at universities is done solo. Most work is done in groups, whether within the formal unit structure, existing committees, or an ad hoc group or task force. Teams can consist of your direct reports, your peers, or committees or task forces. As a leader, you will inherit committees composed of existing membership and a team of direct reports.

The best-case scenario is that all committees are staffed with people who are hard-working, equity-minded, and institutionally focused—meaning that they are focused on the good of the college or the university as a whole, rather than merely their own individual unit. Same for your direct reports: the best case is that you are the final person needed to complete a well-functioning, effective team. We will come back to the topic of committee formation later in this section.

First, let's focus on your team of direct reports. Much as we wish otherwise, it is likely that the team you inherit may not meet the needs of your unit. There will likely be gaps between what exists and what you believe you need. Assuming the relay leg sprint model, you will need to (re)assemble your team quickly. This means a quick assessment of talent—what talent exists and what gaps you need to fill. Talent, or lack thereof, might relate to expertise in content, skills, the ability to relate, ethical challenges, lack of attention to equity, or other issues. You will need to assess the people who compose your team, considering both what you need to get your initiatives done as well as the current talent pool available to accomplish those initiatives. And as you assemble your team, you will need to be clear about your expectations of them, including comportment, interactions, and timelines.

Assessing Existing Talent

To assess existing talent, you typically will have a plethora of secondary data, such as curriculum vitae (CVs) and position descriptions. However, these only tell part of the story. For example, a position description can tell you about the role, but not about how well someone is performing. Likewise, a CV can tell you their previous job titles and the types of institutions they previously worked at, but not the quality of their work. (A CV can also tell you something about their ability to organize thoughts and writing style/ability.)

You don't have to rely solely on the secondary data available. Starting with your interview process, and in all meetings thereafter, you can rely on firsthand observation. Quickly, you will learn who pontificates, who never speaks, and who speaks only when they have something meaningful to contribute. Who procrastinates, and who actually does the work? You should be able to quickly assess the quality of the work someone is doing—and note who is able to complete tasks in a timely way.

Since it is not likely you will start with the team you want and need, you will probably want to make changes. As you think about what types of people you need, keep in mind that groupthink is deadly—it leads to poor process and decisions. You will want people who bring a mix of knowledge, expertise, and skills to the team, and who are willing to say *no* to you and others. Your team, modeled by you, needs to be able to work respectfully through conflicts. Of course, this means they need to have the courage to disagree openly.

As you start your work with the team, as the newest member, keep in mind that it is likely that they have history with one another. Others will know that some of your team are not 'value added,' but they will wait for you to figure it out, and they will wait for you to take action. We found that this was often couched cagily as, "Have you met so-and-so yet? What do you think?" followed by a pause. Few people will tell you outright that someone is not competent. (To explore this and related issues further, you may wish to refer back to Section One, where we discussed the personnel issues you may inherit.)

Start with setting expectations for the team, with all present. You can also set expectations with individuals. Note people's responses to your expectations. As you assess people, trust your instincts. However, at the same time, be careful about your implicit biases. Try to find the assets each person brings and then assign them to tasks or roles that best utilize those assets.

Replacing Team Members

However, there are times when you will need to replace people on your team. Develop a rapid timeline for replacements, if needed. We have found that the natural instinct is to delay the decision; however, in retrospect, we believe that clearing out earlier, if needed, is better.

Process is very important when making these types of replacements on your team. How you take action will both relieve people and scare people. Replacing someone who is known for not doing good work will relieve those who are good workers and will send the message that you have standards and are paying attention. At the same time, replacing people will also scare everyone for the same reason: your action is a reminder that you have standards and are paying attention.

Communication about the decision to replace people is tricky. You must keep confidentiality at the forefront and allow those who are leaving to save face. Under no circumstances should you badmouth them. Discretion and boundaries are important in these situations.

Once you decide to replace someone, you have to quickly decide who will take on their assigned work and how to get that assigned work done. Sometimes, it makes sense to find a replacement in-house, either permanently or pending a search. You will want to look for potential, as it is unlikely you will find others internally who have a proven track record. Consider this a chance to build capacity. Look for opinion leaders; look for those who have the soft skills of gently persuading others, thinking critically, or behaving ethically; look for those who exhibit fairness, reasonableness, integrity, and the ability to keep the institutional view as well as to advocate for their own area. This may seem difficult, but we suspect that someone saw those traits in you and provided opportunities for you to step into leadership roles without the proven track record. If specific knowledge and/or expertise is needed, tell your peers what you are looking for, as they may know the history of others' previous work. The communications office can also provide a list of people with various expertise. We will discuss this in more detail in the next section, 4.2.

Nominating Committee/Task Force Members

As a leader, you will also be asked to nominate people to committees and/or form task forces for specific initiatives. When identifying committee/task force members, you can use some of the same strategies for building your team that we just discussed. Putting people on committees/task forces is a wonderful, typically lower-stakes way to build capacity at your institution. This also provides people the opportunity for leadership so that they can consider whether they wish to pursue more leadership possibilities in the future. We will discuss matching talent to task forces and committees in more detail in Section 4.3.

Later in this section, you can explore the ideas we've discussed further in three case studies:

- The Case of the Amateur Analyst
- The Case of the Public Complaint
- The Case of the Lingering Loafers (Parts A and B)

MICROCONTEXT

1	Of your current team or the team you will inherit, who has which competencies?

2 | Which skills are missing, if any?

SELF-REFLECTION

What are your expectations for your team?

ROADMAP 4.1
How will you communicate your expectations to your team?
To continue assessing your team members: √ Gather secondary data, such as CVs and position descriptions. √ Ask the communications office for an expertise list and review it.

SECTION FOUR: TEAM BUILDING

Case Studies

1. THE CASE OF THE AMATEUR ANALYST

Andy Administrator has been asked to oversee the IR function of the institution. Andy is delighted and has heard high praise about the insights provided by the senior data specialist, Cameron Candid. Andy is also told that Cameron is always learning more, and that Cameron takes courses at the institution each semester, related to the job. Within a month of working with them, Andy notices that Cameron's reports—and conclusions—are based on descriptive data only. When Andy asks for a more sophisticated statistic to be done to answer an urgent question, Andy is surprised to discover that Cameron does not know how to do anything other than descriptive analyses. Andy then finds out that Cameron is taking accounting courses and has never taken a statistics course.

> CONSIDER:
>
> What led to Andy's surprise? Where are the disconnects? What can Andy do now to help make the necessary alignments?
>
> What genders and ethnicities did you imagine about these characters? (How) do any of your answers change based on their intersectional genders and ethnicities, in relation to other characters?

2. The Case of the Public Complaint

President Petry presents a university update at the national alumni meeting, leaving 15 minutes at the end to field questions from the audience. Big Bucks Bentley goes to the mic to ask why the complaints of season ticket holders whose cars were towed at a recent athletic event have not been addressed. The president feels blindsided by hearing about this issue for the first time in a public forum from an alum and board member who is one of the university's biggest donors.

At the next cabinet meeting, the president brings up the topic of creating a digital drop box for all campus complaints. Frankie Fiscal, the CFO, informs the president of an existing drop box for HR, financial, and facilities issues. Newby Nelson, VP for enrollment management, student affairs, and advancement, mentions a similar drop box for student life-related complaints, and Provost Earnest explains the process for academic complaints. The president, not wanting to be blindsided in public again, is unconvinced that separate drop boxes will keep the president's office adequately informed of the numerous complaints the campus receives. Newby tries to emphasize the petty nature of some complaints in their drop box such as "need more salsa choices in the cafeteria on Taco Tuesday," while Frankie shares the serious nature of some employee equity issues in theirs. Clearly, all complaints are not the same, but not wanting to prolong the meeting, one by one, cabinet members agree with the president and leave the meeting to tend to the business of the day. First, however, they have a 'post-meeting' meeting. They realize they did not discuss who will check the box and triage what amount to several hundred complaints a week, but they don't care as long as it's someone else's responsibility. That, they decide, is the president's problem.

> CONSIDER:
>
> What downstream problems will be created by a one-size-fits-all drop box? Describe approaches the cabinet members could have taken to persuade the president to keep the drop boxes separate.

Section Four: Team Building

What issues might this process suggest about the functioning of this senior team?

What genders and ethnicities did you imagine about these characters? (How) do any of your answers change based on their intersectional genders and ethnicities, in relation to other characters?

3A. THE CASE OF THE LINGERING LOAFERS—PART A

Within a few months in the position, Provost Earnest learns fairly quickly that Dean Jolly and Dean Lackey are not following through on any of their College's initiatives, and are barely doing the minimum routine tasks. From Provost Earnest's observation, Dean Jolly just doesn't seem to like to work much, and Dean Lackey is limited by obsequiousness to the College's faculty. Provost Earnest has documented several areas of poor performance in just these few months.

CONSIDER:

Should the provost implement corrective action plans for either/both? How do each of their 'flaws' impact whether or not the deans will follow through on a corrective action plan? If a plan is not likely to yield results, how quickly should the provost replace the dean, and what process should be followed?

What genders and ethnicities did you imagine about these characters? (How) do any of your answers change based on their intersectional genders and ethnicities, in relation to other characters?

3B. THE CASE OF THE LINGERING LOAFERS—PART B

Provost Earnest decided to remove Dean Jolly, given their disinterest in asking for or listening to feedback. The provost worked with HR to offer Jolly a way to step down, and Jolly readily agreed, for a buyout. They collaborated to message the departure, and while Jolly did little work during the interim before leaving, everyone seemed generally pleased with the outcome.

Conversely, Dean Lackey often solicited feedback from the provost (obsequiousness was their nature) and appeared to make some corrections to behavior. However, those corrections were short-lived, and after several months, Dean Lackey reverted back to old patterns. Provost Earnest developed a plan with Dean Lackey about their return to faculty at the end of the academic year, several months away. During that lame-duck time, Dean Lackey had frequent meltdowns in the Deans Council, yelled at the provost during their one-on-one meetings, gave misinformation to the department chairs, and was late in finishing important tasks such as personnel reviews. Provost Earnest also heard from several faculty that Dean Lackey took every opportunity to badmouth the provost to the College's faculty.

> CONSIDER:
>
> Contrast the two approaches. Would you have done anything differently from Provost Earnest? Should the provost have given Dean Jolly more opportunity to improve? Should they have removed Dean Lackey sooner, or were they right in implementing a corrective action plan with the dean?

What genders and ethnicities did you imagine about these characters? (How) do any of your answers change based on their intersectional genders and ethnicities, in relation to other characters?

4.2. Skills and Competencies & Professional Development Needed

> KEY CONCEPTS AND CONSIDERATIONS
>
> - Skills and competencies can be developed and documented in both formal and informal ways.
>
> - Professional development is essential to develop talent, and it can be creatively provided.
>
> - Invest in professional development.
>
> - To build your team and create effective task forces and committees, determine who has skills and competencies, or their potential.
>
> - Use multiple inputs to determine skills and competencies and to match interests and expertise with tasks to be accomplished.

SECTION FOUR: TEAM BUILDING

Overview

As mentioned in the previous section, you will need to find out quickly who has the skills and competencies needed to accomplish your unit's goals. Sometimes you will want people with particular expertise and experience regarding content knowledge. Other times, you may want to forefront those with good 'people' skills and who can contribute good process skills. If there are gaps in either area, you will want to find people to fill them.

Part of your role as leader is to develop and nurture future leaders. Therefore, you will also want to identify who has potential to develop needed skills and competencies. You can also help to build these by supporting a variety of types of professional development opportunities. Identifying both those with current expertise skills and those with potential will enable you to confirm and/or build your team, and will also enable you to create effective committees and task forces.

Identifying Potential Leaders

People's skills and competencies can be documented in both formal and informal ways.

FORMAL METHODS

Formal ways to evaluate who has skills/competencies already include review of their curricula vitae (CV). As mentioned in Section 4.1, their CV can inform you of their range of past experiences, including types of institutions where they have worked. You may want to be cautious about those who have only worked at one institution, which can limit their ability to see the broader view of higher education. Instead, they may have internalized the values and climate, assuming it's the only way to view issues. They may approach all issues with blinders created by working at only one institution.

Also mentioned in Section 4.1 is the expertise list from the communications office. Institutional communications units will often compile a list of expertise, in order to refer the media to resident experts. You can find hidden treasures of skills on those lists, as people have histories prior to their work at the university.

One last formal document mentioned in Section 4.1 is the position descriptions. The same limitations apply here as with CVs—they do not provide an indication of quality—but these descriptions can provide a start in evaluating potential skills.

Take a look at who is in current (or immediate past) leadership in shared governance structures. Who leads the various Senates, or has served as department chair for several terms? These leadership positions may point to people who have good skills and the respect of their colleagues. You will need to assess if the campus climate is such that people only serve in these roles under duress (that is, no one else will volunteer) or if they are truly elected due to respect for their abilities.

Hopefully, you will find good talent in those serving in shared governance leadership or budding talent in those serving as department chairs or unit directors. However, keep in mind the discussion of power dynamics in Section Two. Take note of those who serve in those roles as a boost to their egos, rather than out of a motivation to serve. We have all probably known people in leadership who serve to fuel their narcissism. These are not the people you will want to invite into your trusted team, although there may be roles for them on selected committees and/or task forces.

You may wish to hold regular, formal meetings with those in shared governance leadership to strategize collaborations on initiatives. At one institution, the cabinet could only attend Faculty Senate meetings when invited. This limited the ways in which leadership, particularly the president and provost, could collaborate with them on strategic directions. The president and provost began to hold meetings with the Faculty Senate leadership executive team twice a month, to build relationships and to learn where potential talent lay among the Senate leadership.

INFORMAL METHODS

Some leaders on campus are more hidden. Identifying these leaders will necessitate more informal ways to evaluate who has skills, competencies, and/or potential.

Opinion leaders, as mentioned earlier, are faculty/staff who are respected by their peers. You can often find them by observing interactions during meetings. Note who speaks out and who others do not disagree with, even if they are saying unexpected or untrue things. When these people speak, the room gets quiet—or people build favorably upon what they say.

Develop a list of people who might fit this category. Find ways to connect with them outside of meetings. Go for walks outside your immediate area and stop by for a quick hello. This is not the time for business discussions, but rather, a way to connect personally. These visits are meant to be quick, friendly, and low stakes.

How do you know who has the potential for leadership? These are people who do not yet have experience and who may need to learn the content/knowledge for a position. This is learnable. What is not easily learned or taught is more nuanced. To identify potential, effective leaders, you will want to look for those who have an institutional view. Potential for good leadership includes those who are able to:

- be fair;
- operate from an ethical base;
- demonstrate good process skills, such as facilitation of meetings;
- apply critical thinking to difficult problems; and
- use data well.

If you observe a person with most of these skills, especially during contentious discussions, you have found someone who likely has good leadership potential.

Building Leadership Capacity

Once identified, how do you help these potential leaders grow? You might place them on university-wide committees to build an institutional view and help them to gain experience. Before one of us moved into central administration, we were elected to college-wide personal committees, asked to chair a subcommittee to gather data and write the report for an accreditation standard, and represent the campus at a Board of Trustees meeting for a particular curricular issue.

You can also send those with potential to national conferences to expand their higher-education worldview beyond their one institution. They will then learn the larger status of higher education in the U.S. and be able to see the common concerns across institutions, as well as the unique manifestation of those concerns at your institution. As we were being groomed and trained for leadership, we were sent to the Harvard leadership program. We also attended assessment training at the Higher Learning Commission and the AAC&U institutes as part of campus teams.

As you consider who would benefit from professional development, remember that there is an historical context at the institution for professional development: how it's defined and how its value is perceived. We believe that senior leadership capacity-building relies on professional development. Sending staff and faculty to national conferences about higher education issues is a necessary, but not sufficient in and of itself, way to build capacity and develop leadership potential. Professional development is essential to developing talent, and it can be expensive; sometimes institutions just don't have the resources to send people to national or international conferences. However, those are not the only options. There are creative ways to provide professional development.

During times of revenue shortfalls, institutions sometimes take the short view and delay—or eliminate—investing in professional development. Even if the budget supports investment in professional development, institutions may define PD too narrowly. For example, faculty will often define professional development as conferences within their discipline. Staff may not be supported to attend their professional organizations' conferences.

Ignoring the need for professional development *about* higher education will be more costly to institutions than sending people to conferences. Exposure to the national context of higher education helps potential leaders to learn the common issues faced and the best practices to address them—and breaks down the myth that their institution is unique in facing these challenges. To not send people is to create and/or reinforce an insular and provincial culture that is all too ubiquitous at many institutions, especially at regional comprehensives and smaller private universities.

It can be fairly easy to assess the past and current approach to professional development at your institution. Budgets provide a quick overview of spending and value put on professional development, as do any contractual or policy mandates. This will allow you to see where and how monies are allocated. You can assess what types of professional development are supported, if any. Do faculty only attend conferences in their respective disciplines? Do employees only attend regional or local meetings or conferences? If either is the case, then it suggests a very limited and utilitarian view of professional development.

Based on the above assessment, you can determine the campus climate as it pertains to the need for professional development. To develop leadership capacity, we believe a broader view is needed, one that you might need to advocate in your leadership role. Ask people what they need regarding their own professional development. Based on their responses, your first step might need to be helping them see the value of being part of a national conversation about higher education. You may also need to help your unit, or the institution as a whole, expand their views about the value of professional development.

Even if revenue is very limited, there are some shorter-term, creative ways to support the leadership potential for your institution's employees. Remember,

> **The goals of professional development include discussions of issues more broadly, to understand the macro context for higher education in the twenty-first century, and to help participants learn that the issues facing your institution are likely not unique. Connection with peers—current or future leaders—is also a desired outcome.**

How to do the above without spending a lot of money? Consider providing in-house training and bring the speaker(s) to you. Invite other institutions in the region to participate and share the cost.

When one of us became provost, she sent a team of department chairs to a state conference focused on helping them to develop leadership in that role. The team loved the experience and developed a peer cohort to provide each other with support well beyond the conference. They also brought back some skills and perspectives that they shared with other chairs. Unfortunately, it was cost- and time-prohibitive to send all chairs to the event. It was clear, however, that this would be beneficial for all chairs at that institution, and many of the chairs were asking for similar support. They especially wanted support in developing communication skills as chairs.

To provide this, we planned a one-day workshop with an external speaker who specialized in communication. We collaborated with other provosts in the area, and several agreed to both help underwrite the workshop and invite their chairs to attend. The workshop provided some didactic information but focused mostly on applied. The first half of the day focused on managing and communicating up to deans, and the second half focused on managing and communicating down to faculty in their departments. Chairs from about six other institutions attended.

SECTION FOUR: TEAM BUILDING

The workshop, at a relatively low cost in both money and time, resulted in some skill development in many chairs. By connecting them to colleagues at other institutions, the workshop also gave them a chance to realize that their problems were not unique and that the grass is not always greener elsewhere. In fact, they ended up feeling better about our institution, as they identified some areas in which we were doing well in comparison to others.

This is just one creative way in which professional development can be provided. With the increase in the use of remote synchronous and asynchronous learning, there are many additional ways to support professional development without the travel costs traditionally associated with it. The bottom line is: Invest in professional development for your direct reports and across your sphere of influence in your leadership role. *The benefits will outweigh the costs*; these benefits include development of leadership capacity, morale boosts, and better knowledge and skills in the present.

Later in this section, you can explore these ideas further in two case studies:

- The Case of the Puffed-up Professor
- The Case of the Condescending Committee

MICROCONTEXT

1	What professional development opportunities already exist on campus?

2	What is the campus attitude/climate about professional development?
3	Does the institution invest in sending people for professional development?
4	Are funds allocated for professional development?

Section Four: Team Building

5	Do employees have to pay out-of-pocket? To cover all or part of expenses related to professional development?
6	Are employees attending higher-ed conferences or only those in their discipline, even if in administration?
7	Do employees understand the importance of professional development outside of their discipline?

SELF-REFLECTION

What kinds of informal interactions might you engage in to evaluate who has skills/competencies and/or potential?

SECTION FOUR: TEAM BUILDING

ROADMAP 4.2

How are you going to assess the professional development needs of people in your unit?

Develop a plan for providing for professional development needs that you identify in your unit. Think especially about low-cost ways to meet these needs over the next 1-2 years:

Case Studies

1. THE CASE OF THE PUFFED-UP PROFESSOR

Dr. Dogma is one of the longest-serving faculty on campus, having started their career at this institution. During almost every Senate meeting, Dr. Dogma will contribute to the discussion of any issue at hand. They frequently start with introducing themself as the faculty with the longest time spent at the institution. They consider themself the 'moral compass' of the campus, and consider it their job to protect the campus from straying from what they consider to be ethical actions.

> CONSIDER:
>
> How might Dr. Dogma be helpful to the institution? How might they be harmful to the institution? Do you think people listen to Dr. Dogma? How might their working only at one institution their whole career influence their perspective? What kinds of professional development experiences should Dr. Dogma be encouraged to attend, given that they have been at one institution their entire career?
>
> What genders and ethnicities did you imagine about these characters? (How) do any of your answers change based on their intersectional genders and ethnicities, in relation to other characters?

SECTION FOUR: TEAM BUILDING

2. THE CASE OF THE CONDESCENDING COMMITTEE

Faculty and staff seeking money to pay for professional development submit proposals to a committee, which then reviews and ranks the proposals. It is very competitive, as only about half get funding in any given year. The committee consistently ranks faculty who are presenting scholarship in their discipline higher than those who seek development about the scholarship of teaching and learning, and higher than staff who seek funding to support their development regarding student affairs topics, such as improvement of advising or career services.

CONSIDER:

What does this situation imply about a) how professional development is defined and b) what professional development is valued? Are there any inequities in the current definition/value/process? If Provost Earnest, any of the deans, or HR Director Mona Volador were in a position to influence how professional development is defined, and/or the criteria/process by which funds are allocated, what might they do?

What genders and ethnicities did you imagine about these characters? (How) do any of your answers change based on their intersectional genders and ethnicities, in relation to other characters?

4.3. Matching Talent to Task Forces and Committees

> KEY CONCEPTS AND CONSIDERATIONS
>
> - Heterogeneity is important in membership.
>
> - Process is as important as membership (re: charge to group, shared governance).
>
> - Creation of task forces and committee membership is a leadership development opportunity.

Overview

The first two topics addressed in Section Four focused on building teams and developing talent. In Section 4.3, we will explore the art of creating effective membership composition for task forces and committees. In your leadership role, you will often inherit elected committee members of shared governance groups. Sometimes, you will have the opportunity to make nominations in addition to the elected members, or you may be able to design a task force for a time-limited, specified project. If you have a chance to appoint members, either wholly or in part, here are some ideas to help make the group more functional.

Keep in mind that a good working group will be heterogeneous, composed of people with various content knowledge and interactive skills. You will want to consider both content expertise as well as process needs. You will want some members to bring content expertise; that is, some people will need to have knowledge of the area under study. Others will need to be adept at good process implementation, specifically related to effective organization of ideas. A good group will also have people who are willing to ensure that the process is fair and inclusive of all voices, and who bring good facilitation skills. Try for a mix of perspectives, as well. As mentioned before, quick agreement to solutions will often mean a less than robust group product. A little bit of respectful conflict is helpful for finding better solutions.

The process of how you create the membership is as important as the ultimate member composition. Key tasks include writing a clear charge for the group and using shared governance to inform the nomination process. And, as mentioned before, keep in mind that placing people on various committees and task forces is a great leadership development opportunity.

SECTION FOUR: TEAM BUILDING

The Role of Politics and Power Dynamics

Politics and power dynamics also impact how to create membership on a committee or task force. The larger the scope and impact of the recommendations made, the more political the membership appointments are. You must attend more carefully to the power dynamics in these cases. If the task at hand involves resources, such as personnel allocation or budget, then power dynamics are also relevant.

For example, let's think about a committee whose role is to vet applications for commencement speakers to be given an honorary degree. This fairly low-stakes committee is probably not one in which those in power will want a voice. However, if the committee is one that ranks sabbatical applications and recommends who among their peers might be considered for this time off with pay, politics may be salient. A faculty member without tenure may not be able to easily provide a lower ranking to a senior member of their department who submits a poor application. Committees that make recommendations to approve where resources are allocated are typically high stakes and therefore need members who can withstand criticism and/or scrutiny of recommendations made and processes followed. Also, the more people who are impacted by the recommendation, the more politically fraught it will be. Members of these types of committees need to be empowered, either personally or by title, to be able to participate candidly and ethically on the committee.

Many shared governance committees have prescribed membership. Many positions are elected, but sometimes there are policies for nominations. You may be asked to nominate members. Keep in mind the variables mentioned above. If politics and power dynamics are part of the equation, you may want to solicit self-nominations, and then pick from those. You can also ask for nominations via shared governance.

One of us was tasked with revising the General Education curriculum of the institution. There was an existing shared governance committee, which of course needed to play a key role. However, politically, they were all invested in the current requirements and only represented one College, so they were unlikely to recommend a necessary innovative revision. We decided to form a task force to revise the Gen Ed curriculum, whose membership was to consist of existing Gen Ed committee members as well as appointments from faculty in the other Colleges. The current Gen Ed committee was asked to nominate several of its members to be appointed. In addition, we then invited nominations, via the Faculty Senate, for members from the other Colleges. The process was robust, with disagreements thoughtfully vetted and resolved. The result was a relatively innovative new General Education curriculum, with courses offered from all Colleges across the institution. Subcommittees with members from all Colleges were involved in its implementation.

As with other team building, you can use both formal and informal sources to gather information about possible members for committees and task forces. On the next page, we will also discuss how to evaluate the politics and power dynamics of committee appointments.

Evaluating Potential Appointments

As mentioned above, with all of the aforementioned caveats, formal sources include people's curriculum vitae (CV), job descriptions, and the expertise list developed by the institutional communications office. For some tasks, having direct experience is important. One of our institutions needed a revision of all the promotion and tenure policies and formed a task force to make recommendations for these revisions. Membership in this case was limited to people who had been through the tenure process and who had been promoted at least once. Politically, it was also important that those who made these recommendations had some standing and the respect of their peers.

You may also wish to consider how to include members who hold more informal types of influence. Opinion leaders are useful for important committee work, especially those who may offer vocal opposition to potential changes. Dealing with conflictual issues early lends itself to a better outcome. They will bring up legitimate concerns (sometimes non-legitimate ones, too). At least those concerns will be on the table to address, and if these are resolved, this will lead to better solutions. Those who are opponents initially, if invited to become invested in a process that they participate in, can often become visible cheerleaders for recommended changes. The key is to involve them from the beginning.

Let's examine politics a bit more and assess when you might want to attend more to those dynamics when selecting committee or task force members. As you get to know your new institution, notice whether the same few people serve on every important committee. They may assume it's their right to serve and be the voice for their constituency. Some people may think they 'own' an issue—so weigh the pros and cons of putting them on the committee. Do you want to reinforce their 'ownership' or get new voices involved? It depends on your assessment of the value of either. You may also want to assess who does not serve on committees in general, and why. It may be that service and committee work at the institution is not valued. Or, if work is done, the recommendations are rarely acted on. Both of these situations would discourage wide involvement.

If the same few serve, the institution may benefit from a frank discussion about the lack of willingness to serve. How important is it to 'spread the wealth' in committee service? All of these issues create a micro context for the politics of service at an institution.

As mentioned above, you will want to match the appointments to the politics of the task. Tasks of smaller scope may use less senior people. This helps to expose junior faculty or staff to their growing edge of learning and helps them to develop a wider view. Decide if this is a good opportunity to build someone into leadership, while protecting junior people from areas that are overly political. Tasks of smaller scope can help to introduce less senior people to leadership possibilities. However, if the task involves recommendations that will impact a large number of people and that are important, you will want to use opinion leaders. Remember to include at least one person who holds a skeptical or oppositional view to bring their ideas and influence into the process, and ultimately, into the final decision(s) or recommendations.

Before you nominate someone, be sure to let them know of your intent to do so. Some people, no matter their seniority, may not realize what they have to offer. In building capacity, you may see their potential, even if they don't. We have found that many people are willing to do the work, when asked. When you approach them, be ready with specific examples of the skills and expertise they will bring to the work. Many are pleased to be asked and will do their best to live up to the talent you observed and named.

Writing the Charge

Lastly, there is an art to writing the charge. Formal, ongoing committees sometimes need to have their charge revisited. Task forces designed for a limited project will also need a clearly crafted charge. If you are tasked to write a charge, first and foremost, it needs to be clear and parsimonious. Include the expectation of the use of data to inform their recommendations—and specify the kind of data. The type of data will be dictated by the task at hand. If the task force is formed to design initiatives about student retention, you might request a literature review. Consider if the task would benefit from quantitative or descriptive data, or both. Decide if the Institutional Research office will provide the data, or if the task force or committee will need to gather it. We have found it useful to ask the committee/task force what data they need and help them to locate it, or provide it, if possible. Embedding the requirement to use data in the charge helps with creating and reinforcing a data-supported decision making model (see Section Five). This also helps ground the work in something besides just members' opinions.

The charge to the group should also include a timeline and deliverables. Be clear whether they are making recommendations (typically to the one who writes the charge) or if they are the decision makers about any aspect of the task at hand. (Refer to the activity in Section 3.3—page 156—as well as the activity later in this section—page 197—for more on writing the charge.)

Later in this section, you can explore these ideas further in this case study:

- The Case of the Preferential Personnel Process

MICROCONTEXT

1	What committees exist on campus? Are they active? Do they submit reports? Do they have written goals or necessary functions? Do they publish their meeting schedule and minutes from past meetings?
2	Assess how service on committees/task forces is viewed on campus.
3	Assess whether the same few people serve on every important committee. If the 'usual suspects always serve,' what does that imply concerning the climate about service?

Section Four: Team Building

4 | Assess who doesn't serve, and why.

5 | Assess how important it is to 'spread the wealth' regarding service on committees/task forces.

6 | In creating task forces/committees:

    a. What can you tell from formal docs, such as CVs and job descriptions?

b. Are there areas of expertise that might help with any given task?

7 Who are the opinion leaders among the faculty? Among staff?

8 Who *expects* to be included in 'important' work?

SECTION FOUR: TEAM BUILDING

9 | How and when might you want to involve 'junior' people to help them to develop into larger leadership roles?

SELF-REFLECTION

Who do you tend to put on committees? Are these people you know well, or do you include people not known to you?

Whom do you trust to inform your decisions about committee/task force creation?

SECTION FOUR: TEAM BUILDING

Activity

SELECTING A TASK FORCE

For the Activity in Section 3.3, you wrote the charge. Now that you have written the charge, pick **seven** people to serve on the task force. For this Activity:

- Refer to the Appendix and choose from the list of Case Study characters.
- Keep in mind the Microcontext questions on the preceding pages.
- You will also want to consider a mix of people who might bring vocal opposition and people with the expertise needed, as well as opinion leaders, related to the task at hand.

YOUR TASK FORCE	
1. _____	5. _____
2. _____	6. _____
3. _____	7. _____
4. _____	

Notes:

Case Study

1. THE CASE OF THE PREFERENTIAL PERSONNEL PROCESS

President Petry is concerned that when alumni apply for jobs on campus, few, if any, are hired. The president submits a policy revision to the policy committee, which asks them to consider adding preferential language to the personnel process. The policy language would provide alumni job candidates with automatic consideration as a finalist for any position for which they are qualified. The policy does not mandate they are hired, only that, if qualified, they are able to be among the finalists in the interview process. The president runs this by Faculty Senate leadership first, and Abby Monkson supports it. However, when vetted in the Policy Committee and the full Faculty Senate, the proposed policy revision is defeated for recommendation forward.

> CONSIDER:
>
> What are the politics involved in this situation, from the perspectives of alumni, advancement, faculty, staff, and Board of Trustees? Was this a reasonable policy change request by the president? Were there any other processes needed to increase the likelihood of the policy being recommended?
>
> What genders and ethnicities did you imagine about these characters? (How) do any of your answers change based on their intersectional genders and ethnicities, in relation to other characters?

SECTION FIVE:
ESSENTIALS OF SHARED GOVERNANCE

1. Creating or Reinforcing a Culture of Data-Supported Decision Making
2. Budget and Resource Allocation
3. Assessment and Accreditation
4. Intersecting Purviews

Shared governance can create a collegial, productive work environment *or* result in a situation where faculty, staff, students, and administrators are at constant odds with each other in unproductive ways. To create the former and reduce the likelihood of the latter, senior leaders need to skillfully negotiate different stakeholder perspectives on important issues such as the use of data, budget and resource allocation, and assessment and accreditation.

Section Five begins by focusing on increasing transparency and a sense of shared responsibility by creating or reinforcing a culture of data-supported decision making, followed by a focus on one of the most misunderstood components of university operations—budget and finance. This section also explores how to frame assessment and accreditation in a way that emphasizes continuous improvement of the student experience or administrative operations, instead of approaching them as perfunctory compliance exercises. This section then closes with a discussion of the use of data and documentation in the consultative process.

5.1. Creating or Reinforcing a Culture of Data-Supported Decision Making

"If we have data, let's go with that. If all we have are opinions, let's go with mine." —Jim Barksdale

---

KEY CONCEPTS AND CONSIDERATIONS

- Data-supported decision making focuses attention on what needs to be done to achieve desired outcomes.
- Data-supported decision making increases transparency.
- Data-supported decision making is everyone's responsibility.

Data Supported Decision Making (DSDM) Basics

One of the most surprising things about higher education is the lack of data-supported decision making that exists on many campuses. New academic programs are launched without conducting market demand or competitive analysis. Semester after semester, classes are scheduled with no data regarding student availability and without using algorithms that can speed time to graduation. Services are provided to students and employees based on past history rather than current needs or use of evidence-based practices. Even in situations where data is available, it is not used consistently to make decisions. It is up to you as a leader to require your team to make data-supported decisions, and you must set the example by presenting data for the decisions you make.

So how are most decisions made on your campus? Are they based on data? If not, are they based on what is called HIPPOs—the Highest-Paid Person's Opinion? HIPPO decisions become the fallback position for several reasons. In some cases, HIPPO decisions occur when adequate data may not be available. To remedy that situation, work with your institution's chief data officer for the collection and analysis of data you need in order to make both routine and strategic decisions for your unit.

Another situation that leads to HIPPO decisions occurs when your direct reports allow decisions to default to you, using the excuse that the decisions are "above my pay grade." Do not allow this to happen to you. Hold your direct reports accountable for making decisions that are within their level of authority, using the best data available. DSDM will never become the norm on campus if only those in senior leadership positions are expected to use data while everyone else relies on hunches, or worse, while they fall back on what is called TWWADI.

What is TWWADI? It stands for "the way we always do it." Let us think about this for a minute. Why should a campus or unit bother to assemble a strategic planning committee to spend several months writing an elaborate strategic plan, invest thousands of dollars printing it in full color on glossy paper, organize and hold kickoff events and develop press releases to launch a strategic plan, just to continue to fall back on the same old hunches and routines to operate the campus? TWWADI is the reason that some strategic plans are neither strategic nor plans.

As a senior leader, you should ask to join your institution's data governance and/or data analytics council. This will help to ensure the data you need is correctly defined, collected, and appropriately analyzed to aid in the proper functioning and evaluation of your unit. Participation in your campus's data governance body or analytics council will give you the opportunity to understand and influence data ownership policies and to have input into the accuracy and assumptions about data creation. You will also gain clarity regarding authority, data sourcing, and data security, as well as get ahead of potential changes to the institution's enterprise resource planning (ERP) system.

LIVE VS. HISTORICAL DATA

Working with the data governance body or analytics council, you will also learn about access to and the uses of live (or real-time) data and frozen (or historical) data. Both can be used for decision making for different purposes.

Live, or *real-time, data* is produced in your campus's ERP and analytics systems every day and can be used to gauge the effectiveness of activities in real time. For example, online student recruitment campaigns that encourage prospects to visit a website to inquire about enrollment can be monitored in real time. Further, the choice architecture can be altered with minimal lag-time, if necessary, to encourage the desired action from prospective students.

Frozen, or *historical data,* is typically collected less frequently and is used to review trends over time for actions or activities that take place on a monthly, semester, or annual basis, such as course enrollments. Frozen data is generally used for developing official reports, accreditation, and submissions to state and federal agencies. It can also be used to review the impact of policies, business practices, and student success initiatives.

SHADOW SYSTEMS

A quick word about shadow systems. In some cases, units collect their own data, typically on spreadsheet software, which may or may not be aligned with campus data governance policies and definitions for official institutional data. Be careful when using data from shadow systems held by other units and your own. It can be used to collect and report items specific to your unit, such as attendance at unit-sponsored events, but should not be used for official institutional reports. As recommended earlier, request to participate in your institution's data governance and/or data analytics council so that the data your unit needs is collected as official data.

Data Democratization

> **To the extent possible, every employee at all levels of the institution should have access to data for decision making.**

You can create this for your own unit, even if it's not possible at the institutional level. Everyone should be held accountable for acting on data-supported decisions, with ongoing evaluation of outcomes to determine if things are going in the right direction. If they are not, collect data to help you diagnose the problem and course correct. We mentioned this kind of accountability earlier when we discussed creating charges for task forces and committees that require the use of data.

A transparent method of DSDM involves using campus-wide data dashboards to present information needed to make decisions and evaluate your unit's performance.

One of us joined an institution that had numerous data analytics tools and well-developed data governance. Despite these assets, the consistent use of data was limited to a few people and a few units. To remedy this, a data democratization project was initiated to provide live data, in the aggregate, to all employees. Leadership had to set the example if DSDM was to become the norm on campus; the executive dashboard, which was updated daily, was made available to all employees. When meetings were held, whether one-on-one or in large groups, data from the executive dashboard could be used to discuss important and difficult decisions that needed to be made to move the institution forward. The CIO and IT team held ongoing data analytics training to make sure all employees had the opportunity to learn how to access the dashboards, run reports, and arrive at insights to help them make the best routine and strategic decisions.

Without democratized data, it will be very difficult to create and maintain a culture of data-supported decision making and radical transparency (see Section 6.1). Make sure all members of your team have access to and training to utilize unit- or campus-wide dashboards, both live and historical, and annual reports. Below are some suggestions for moving your institution/unit towards data democratization.

RECOMMENDATIONS FOR MOVING TOWARD DSDM

- At the institutional level, assemble an applied analytics task force consisting of chief data and chief information officers and functional users. Develop campus-wide communications to inform all parties about the purpose of the data review and ask for their participation and cooperation. Ensure final task force findings and recommendations are shared campus wide.
- At the unit level, form a data analytics team to suggest the types and use of data for making routine and strategic decisions.
- Provide or seek ongoing professional development for team members on the use of data tools and DSDM.
- Hold unit-level "Data Days" to review and update data and to encourage the use of data to make decisions.
- Require that all written requests for resources be accompanied by official institutional data (not data from shadow systems).

To learn more about DSDM and related topics, peruse the online library of Educause (www.educause.edu), an organization dedicated to innovative uses of information technology in higher education. Gartner, an international research and consulting firm (www.gartner.com), also has a wealth of information regarding all things IT across all industries, including the latest research on data and analytics strategies.

Later in this section, you can explore these ideas further in this case study:

- The Case of the Swelling Student Body

SECTION FIVE: ESSENTIALS OF SHARED GOVERNANCE

MICROCONTEXT

1. Describe the extent to which a culture of data-supported decision-making exists on the campus:

2. How are most decisions made on your campus?

3. Are there certain decisions that are based on data and others that are not?

4	Are there decisions that are based on what are called HIPPOs—the highest paid person's opinion? If so, which decisions are made this way?
5	Are there areas that use and produce good data and areas that do not?
6	Describe data governance on your campus. Is there a data governance body? Do they have written processes?

Section Five: Essentials of Shared Governance

| 7 | What data is official, who owns that data, and which office is the official repository for the unit/campus? |

| 8 | Do all employees have access to data for making routine and strategic decisions? What do they have access to? What do they need access to? |

| 9 | Where are there pockets of shadow data within your unit or in areas that impact the data you use to make decisions? |

| 10 | What unit on campus provides applied data analytics training? What training is available? |

SELF-REFLECTION
When do you use live data vs. frozen data?

Under what circumstances might it be acceptable for you to make HIPPO decisions for your unit?

Do you have any concerns about sharing your unit's data with the campus?

Earlier we spoke about information as power. Would you feel uncomfortable or somehow exposed to open up your unit's data to the campus? If so, why?

If you feel perfectly comfortable sharing your unit's data campus-wide, is there anyone inside or outside your unit who would give you pushback? If so, why?

SECTION FIVE: ESSENTIALS OF SHARED GOVERNANCE

ROADMAP 5.1

First:

√ Inquire about and join your institution's data governance and/or data analytics council.

Then:

What data sources exist for your unit and the campus?

Plan ongoing training for your team members to make routine and strategic decisions with data:

Plan to hold unit-level "Data Days" to review and update data and encourage the use of data to make decisions:

Case Study

1. THE CASE OF THE SWELLING STUDENT BODY

Andy Administrator leads the institutional research office and is tasked with assembling official university data to inform a program prioritization process. A series of town hall meetings is scheduled to discuss the process and review the data. At the second meeting, Andy presents enrollment data for all academic programs. Andy is peppered with skeptically framed questions at the end of the presentation, and every department chair in attendance disputes the number of students seeking degrees in their academic programs. To help settle the dispute, President Petry asks academic departments to submit their numbers to compare to the institution's official report. When the totals submitted by departments are summed up, the grand total is three times greater than the number of students who paid tuition.

CONSIDER:

What could cause such a large discrepancy between the official institutional enrollment numbers and the total submitted by departments?

What should be discussed at the next town hall meeting? Who should lead the discussion? Andy or the president?

What genders and ethnicities did you imagine about these characters? (How) do any of your answers change based on their intersectional genders and ethnicities, in relation to other characters?

5.2. Budget and Resource Allocation

"A budget tells us what we can't afford, but it doesn't keep us from buying it." —William Feather

> KEY CONCEPTS AND CONSIDERATIONS
>
> - All parties should understand the distinction between how the institution is financed and how annual budgets are determined.

Overview

One of the most misunderstood components of university operations is budget and finance. This lack of clarity can be attributed, in some cases, to fear of open and honest discussion that might reveal the tenuous nature of the financial situation of the university, as revenue is eclipsed by the growth of expenses.

Some of the most emotionally charged meetings at a university involve the discussion of budgeting and resource allocation. The tone that some leaders use to communicate at these meetings is often at opposite ends of the spectrum—either *doom and gloom* or *placating and patronizing*. Neither tone aids in shedding light on the university's true financial situation, the budgeting process, and the appropriate path forward given some of the financial challenges an institution faces.

Quite often, even employees who are members of the university budget committee have only a vague understanding of how the university is financed, how budgets are determined, and how resources are allocated. Given that the budget can be a proxy for a university's unspoken priorities, make sure that not only do you understand the budget of the institution and your unit, but that your staff members understand it as well. Be aware of your expenditures and have a clear picture of the revenue sources for your institution, the direct or indirect role your unit plays in revenue generation, and the source of funds or financing for your unit.

So, if 'doom and gloom' and 'placating and patronizing' are the wrong ways to discuss budget issues, what is a better way for you as a senior leader to have difficult conversations with your team when budgets are cut or reallocated? Below are some suggestions:

HOLDING DIFFICULT CONVERSATIONS ABOUT BUDGETS AND RESOURCE ALLOCATION

- Never discuss cuts or reallocations until you have a full, data-informed picture of the situation. To do otherwise can be misleading and unnecessarily stressful for all parties. If pressed, inform your team that you will share what you know when you have fact-based information (not rumors) and are authorized to communicate to them, as some information may be embargoed.

- Keep your messaging brief and focused on the broad, institutional perspective.

- Refrain from editorializing, blaming, and name-calling. Saying the budget cut is BS, attributing shortfalls to the poor performance of other units, and calling the CFO or president a cheapskate will not change the balance sheet, but it will make you look petty and unprofessional. Although it is difficult, take responsibility for those decisions that are yours. Blaming those 'higher up' the chain will undercut your authority.

- Make the budget a periodic agenda item to help lessen the surprise of bad news and to lift the spirits of your team when things change for the better.

The Enrollment Cliff

Now, a brief discussion of the *enrollment cliff*, a phenomenon that will occur between 2025 and 2029 due to the significant decrease in the traditional college-age population, 18 to 22, caused by the decline in the U.S. fertility rate.[4] You've read about it. You've talked about it. What are you going to do about it? Do you think it is someone else's problem? Think again. The largest percentage of annual revenue for most campuses is tuition and fees. For this reason, it is in the interest of all campus units that enough students are recruited, enrolled, and retained until graduation to help cover institutional operating costs. How your unit's functions directly or indirectly impact student enrollment must be a frequent topic for your staff meetings. Student recruitment and academic success is everyone's responsibility.

Likewise, you and your team should learn all you can about higher education budget and financial issues. For detailed and comprehensive information, visit the website of the National Association of College and University Business Officers (NACUBO) at www.nacubo.org, an excellent resource for all things financial in higher education. Take advantage of their publications, workshops, and podcasts to gain a greater understanding of budget concepts and to stay abreast of financial and regulatory issues affecting higher education.

Later in this section, you can explore these ideas further in two case studies:

- The Case of the Goldilocks Grid
- The Case of the Competitive Process

MICROCONTEXT

1	How is the institution/unit financed?

---

[4] See Missy Kline's "The Looming Higher Ed Enrollment Cliff," *Higher Ed HR Magazine,* CUPA-HR, Fall 2019: https://www.cupahr.org/issue/feature/higher-ed-enrollment-cliff.

Section Five: Essentials of Shared Governance

2. How tuition-dependent is your campus budget? What other alternate revenue sources are there, and how limited are they?

3. What percent of the budget is restricted vs. unrestricted?

4. What percentage of the budget is fixed cost?

5	How much of the fixed cost is salary and wages?
6	How much of the fixed cost is for infrastructure?
7	What percentage of the annual budget is for the academic division vs. non-academic divisions?

SECTION FIVE: ESSENTIALS OF SHARED GOVERNANCE

8 | Has your campus calculated a break-even point? If so, what is it? Above and beyond the cost of instruction, how much goes to overhead?

9 | How are annual budgets determined for the institution and for its units?

10 | What is the resource allocation process for new units or new academic programs?

| 11 | Has the institution conducted a program prioritization process for all units? If so, how were the results used? |

| 12 | Is there a performance funding component for the institution and for its units? If so, describe: |

| 13 | Over the past three years, is there a trend of a budget deficit or a surplus? |

Section Five: Essentials of Shared Governance

| 14 | How are budget cuts handled? Are they across the board, or is there a prioritization process? |

| 15 | Is there proactive planning for things like deferred maintenance in the event of budget shortfalls? |

| 16 | What is the most recent estimate of deferred maintenance? |

17	How much money is set aside annually to address deferred maintenance?
18	How much is in the reserve fund?
19	Is the Higher Education Price Index used for financial planning?

SECTION FIVE: ESSENTIALS OF SHARED GOVERNANCE

20	Are budgets for academic units aligned with student enrollments in academic programs?
21	Does the institution participate in the Delaware Cost Study? If so, how are findings used?
22	How is return on investment or value-added evaluated for academic and non-academic units?

| 23 | Are budgeting models updated with strategic plans? |

SELF-REFLECTION
How prepared are you to make difficult and/or unpopular decisions for your unit during financial downturns?

SECTION FIVE: ESSENTIALS OF SHARED GOVERNANCE

ROADMAP 5.2

Calculate the return on investment or value-added for your unit:

Make a plan to align your budget to your priorities:

> After aligning your budget and priorities, determine if you need more resources and make a plan to request them:

Case Studies

1. The Case of the Goldilocks Grid

Provost Earnest needed data to allocate a handful of faculty positions for the upcoming year; via the deans, the provost had received twenty requests for five possible positions!

Earnest was able to compile data to create a scatter plot:

- On the x axis, the data indicated the cost per number of majors per program.
- On the y axis, the data indicated the cost per student FTE per program.
- Each intersecting data point provided a semi-complete indication of the cost efficiency of each program.

Provost Earnest also superimposed the 'break even' line on each axis, which let them know which programs were under-resourced, over-resourced, or just about right. They shared this scatterplot with the faculty and deans as a way to provide transparency about their allocation decisions. The faculty who did not receive positions nicknamed this 'the gruesome graph.'

Section Five: Essentials of Shared Governance

CONSIDER:

Why did Provost Earnest use this data to help inform their decisions? Did they omit other data that was equally important? What might have led faculty to nickname this graph in the way they did? Was there anything else the provost might have done regarding the transparency of their decision?

What genders and ethnicities did you imagine about these characters? (How) do any of your answers change based on their intersectional genders and ethnicities, in relation to other characters?

2. The Case of the Competitive Process

After three years of an (unfortunately accurate) predicted deficit budget, President Petry decided that the campus needed a program prioritization process. Petry hired a consultant, who met with all constituencies on campus and set up a process. Both faculty and staff were involved in writing reports and reviewing all the data. The entire campus was kept informed. At the end of the year, the institution had a report that created five categories of programs/units (both academic and administrative), ranging from those that needed resources and those that needed specific improvements, to those that needed to be eliminated.

However, there were no resources to allocate other than the ones freed up from eliminations. Ultimately, one year later, only a handful of administrative units were eliminated. The three academic programs targeted for sunsetting were fiercely protected and remained untouched. Rifts between faculty developed, and some were never mended. The budget deficit was cut by half during the first year post-process, and by year two, was almost break-even.

> CONSIDER:
>
> What was President Petry's intent? Did President Petry's timing for the program prioritization process impact the results, and in what way? Were the results largely successful or unsuccessful? Is there anything Petry might have done differently?
>
> Would Petry have done better with across-the-board budget cuts?

What genders and ethnicities did you imagine about these characters? (How) do any of your answers change based on their intersectional genders and ethnicities, in relation to other characters?

5.3. Assessment and Accreditation

"Improvement in post-secondary education will require converting teaching from a solo sport to a community-based research activity." —Herbert A. Simon

> KEY CONCEPTS AND CONSIDERATIONS
>
> - Accreditation and assessment should be used to add value and not just for compliance.

More than Just Compliance

Leaders in the higher education industry are held accountable to students, parents, politicians, and each other. It's no longer okay to rest on the assumption of value; we need data to validate value.

All institutions have some kind of evaluations for academic and operational processes, which include accreditations and strategic planning. Most also engage in assessment of student learning. However, the campus climate concerning the assessment of student learning and program accreditations or reviews will influence work in these areas. Cynical attitudes toward assessment and accreditations can result in perfunctory efforts that miss the opportunity to engage in the process in a way that continuously improves the student experience or administrative operations.

Institutional Accreditation

As you start in a leadership role, note where the institution is in its accreditation cycle. Find out if there are important follow-up items that need to be addressed and if your unit is involved. Determine how findings from accreditation visits—both institutional and discipline-focused—are used. (Or are they?) And if there are repeat audit issues related to your unit, take steps to make permanent corrections to improve important broken functions and avoid future audit findings.

Assessments and accreditations are time-consuming and involve considerable effort, and they can fill the hearts of faculty and staff with dread. As a leader, it is your job to find ways to make the processes and outcomes valuable beyond the external pressure to engage in them. You may need to take part in a cheerleading function to help the campus see and embrace the value of these processes. Additionally, not everyone is aware of the resource implications of institutional accreditation—a requirement for receiving Title IV funding from the federal government. You may need to work with other leaders to help the campus community understand this important requirement.

Assessment of Student Learning

Accreditations can be used to garner resources. Assessment of student learning, on the other hand, is often viewed as a necessary evil and is conducted begrudgingly. In some cases, faculty will want to make assessment of student learning more complex than necessary, if they agree to do it at all. If you are responsible for an academic unit, make sure assessments of student learning use empirical data and close the loop—that is, that they use the data collected to improve student learning.

Program-Level Accreditations

Program-level accreditations are often considered a coveted signal of program quality. While faculty may find them important for program reputation and for requesting resources, they may have limited value in student recruitment, depending on the field. Institutions should not rush to a decision when considering program-level accreditations. They should weigh the pros and cons of seeking new accreditations for programs; their attainment and maintenance is very resource-intensive.

Internal Program Review

Many campuses have established an internal program review cycle for academic programs and administrative units. Optimally, results of internal reviews can be used for continuous improvement, going beyond the ubiquitous requests for resources. If your institution does not have an internal program review cycle, this may be something you want to introduce.

When designing the process, be sure to include:

- A schedule for the frequency of reviews
- A template about areas to cover (with a page limit)
- Clear expectations for use of data
- Clarity about how the results will be used for continuous improvement and resource allocation

Strategic Plans

Strategic plans, a university mainstay, are typically neither strategic nor plans. Too often, these documents are underfunded wish lists, developed separately and apart from accreditation and assessment data. Strategic plans *should* be informed by accreditation and assessment data, but when accreditation and assessment are considered a nuisance and are performed as an obligatory assignment, these will have limited ability to shape a meaningful strategic plan.

Later in this section, you can explore these ideas further in two case studies:

- The Case of the Impassioned Plea
- The Case of the Consequential Karma

MICROCONTEXT

1	What is the current climate regarding accreditation/assessment at your institution?
2	In what stage of the accreditation cycle is the institution/unit?
3	Are there any follow-up items from previous accreditation reviews? How are the results used?

Section Five: Essentials of Shared Governance

4	What is the academic climate regarding assessment? Does it vary from department to department?
5	Is there an academic review cycle? What is the academic program review cycle and process? Are they used for continuous improvement beyond additional resource requests?
6	How frequently are labor market analytics used to update curricular and co-curricular offerings to enhance the employability of students?

7	What is the climate regarding assessment of non-academic units? Does it vary from office to office?
8	Is there a periodic review process for non-academic units? If so, are these reviews used for continuous improvement beyond additional resource requests?
9	Are there new or repeat audit issues that the institution/unit needs to address?

Section Five: Essentials of Shared Governance

10	Do all academic and selected non-academic units have goals that align with university-wide student learning outcomes? What measures are used?
11	Do all non-academic units have goals that support student success inside and/or outside the classroom? What measures are used?
12	How does your unit contribute to university-wide learning outcomes?

13	How are the findings from any/all of the assessments/accreditations/evaluations used to inform planning and/or continuous improvement and/or resource allocation on campus (formally or informally)?
14	Are there any open HR issues that need immediate attention?
15	Are there any open legal issues that need immediate attention?

SECTION FIVE: ESSENTIALS OF SHARED GOVERNANCE

16	Are there any open local, state, or federal compliance issues that need immediate attention?
17	Are there any open issues in the athletics department that need immediate attention (if applicable)?
18	Are there any open student life issues that need immediate attention?

| 19 | Are there any open physical plant and safety issues that need immediate attention? |

SELF-REFLECTION

Have you been a cheerleader for a process or initiative that you did or did not agree with? How did you craft your message to support the institution's goals?

SECTION FIVE: ESSENTIALS OF SHARED GOVERNANCE

ROADMAP 5.3

First:

√ Obtain a calendar of accreditations and determine: Do you or your unit have a role?

√ Review your unit's goals to ensure they align with institutional goals.

Then:

Look for areas of improvement that are often mentioned repeatedly in assessments/accreditations/evaluations but are not addressed. Determine who should be responsible for 'fixing' them and, if they fall under your portfolio, delegate:

Case Studies

1. THE CASE OF THE IMPASSIONED PLEA

Professor Mensch, an associate professor in the Languages Department, works hard. The professor is an excellent teacher, does whatever service is asked of them, and produces good scholarship. While in a meeting with Dean Outsider, who is discussing plans for assessment of student learning and institutional accreditation, Professor Mensch blurts out, "Why can't they just trust us? We do a good job!"

> CONSIDER:
>
> How might Dean Outsider respond to Professor Mensch's statement, focusing on the microcontext? How might the dean use the opportunity to help those in the meeting understand the importance of both assessment and accreditation in higher education in the 21st century?
>
> What genders and ethnicities did you imagine about these characters? (How) do any of your answers change based on their intersectional genders and ethnicities, in relation to other characters?

2. THE CASE OF THE CONSEQUENTIAL KARMA

Dr. Dogma has insisted for a decade, on principle, that their department, part of the liberal arts tradition, will not do programmatic assessment of student learning; Dr. Dogma claims that assigning grades in classes is sufficient and that learning in their discipline is not measurable in any other way. The department's major is very small, and they serve an important role in the general education curriculum. The department has had several faculty retirements in the last couple of years and is asking for one new tenure-track position. Unfortunately, the data required to justify the position includes student learning assessment data, which they cannot provide.

CONSIDER:

How might Dean Lackey handle this position request, since it lacks the required data? Is there an opportunity to impact Dr. Dogma's refusal to assess student learning at the programmatic level?

What genders and ethnicities did you imagine about these characters? (How) do any of your answers change based on their intersectional genders and ethnicities, in relation to other characters?

Activity

Your unit's programs (non-accredited academic and operational units) are not evaluated periodically. Use the template provided below to establish a process.

TEMPLATE FOR ESTABLISHING AN INTERNAL PROGRAM AND DEPARTMENTAL REVIEW PROCESS

Below are guidelines for each part of the development of the plan.

A. Introduction

- Provide a context for these processes.

- Provide a general description of the overall process, including who oversees it, its ties to your regional accreditor, and the items contained in the document.

- Differentiate between academic department reviews and administrative unit reviews, and their processes. Clarify that this process exists outside of external accreditation.

- Consider the following as some possible purposes for this process:

    1. Thoughtful self-assessment and planning of future direction.

    2. Evaluation of the department's current status (since the last review) and overall quality including staff, resources, effectiveness, and identification of future opportunities for growth and improvement.

    3. Setting strategic goals and recommendations for actions to maximize effectiveness of the department, and alignment of resources.

- Describe the consequences for resources upon completion, or the lack of access if it is not completed.

- Provide a list of programs that will be reviewed, divided between academic and administrative departments. Do not include programs that are externally accredited, and be inclusive of all professional departments, including Academic Affairs, the Office of the President, etc. Include degrees/programs offered that may be in departments that have external accreditation as a whole, but which are not included under it. (See the sample timeline, below, for examples.)

B. Process

1. Orient Department Under Review:

- Describe the orientation process. Who will meet with the department? When? What will be discussed in general?

2. Self-Study Preparation and Department Responsibilities:

- Describe the self-study requirements. What information/input from constituencies is expected? What data will be provided by IR? What is covered in the narrative? What is the page limit for the narrative? (*Tip:* Set a page limit!) Describe what goes in the narrative and what would be considered appendices to the self-study.
- Describe to whom to send the report for feedback and review prior to the final version. This will likely include the direct supervisor, the assessment coordinator, the university-wide assessment committee, and the people in the division that oversees the assessment coordinator.

3. Review Committee:

- Describe the shared governance assessment/program review committee. Describe how a subcommittee of its members will be assigned for each review. (*Tip*: No more than three—including two from the type of area under review and one from the 'other side of the house.')
- Describe the purpose of the review committee: *to validate and clarify the self-study*. Once they receive the self-study, how might they do this, including requesting more or different data? What meetings might occur with the department under review?
- Describe the report to be produced by the review committee, including a page limit. To whom is it submitted?
- Define completion of their work.

4. Post Review:

- Describe whom the program under review will meet with to finalize the process. This may include their immediate supervisor and the divisional vice president/provost. Describe to whom the final recommendations are sent, and the role of the president, if any.
- Describe expectations about annual tracking toward goals set based on the review.

Appendices A and B. Sample Academic Department and Professional Department Self-Study Outlines

As appendices, provide an outline of expected sections for a self-study document for both academic departments and administrative departments:

- Include instructions for maximum page length and format (e.g., double-spaced). Specify whether or not the limit includes cover page/appendices.
- Include a list of all sections for self-study.

Appendix C. Sample Timeline and Rotation

Units under review will typically first meet approximately x months prior to the deadline of their review process (provide at least a year, probably longer). Provide this as an appendix:

- Differentiate between a fall and a spring timeline. Provide a sample timeline for each, starting with the initial orientation meeting and concluding with post-review recommendation meetings.
- Decide how often each program will undergo review. (Typically, five to seven years provides a reasonable rotation, given the work involved and the time needed to accomplish goals.)
- Decide how many programs to review each year. Define a balance between academic and administrative programs.

5.4. Intersecting Purviews

> KEY CONCEPTS AND CONSIDERATIONS
>
> - The consultation process must be documented and clarified with data, budget requests, and resource implications.

Overview

Consultation with faculty, staff, and students can be formally required in university policies or informally requested by shared governance leaders. What is generally missing, however, are details of what constitutes consultation. (We discussed this earlier in Section 3.3.) Consultation is intended to add value to the decision making process by bringing different perspectives to the table. We recommend that the consultation process be documented and clarified with data, budget requests, and resource implications in order to ensure that stakeholder input adds value, not just opposition, to the process.

DSDM

As a leader who uses data to make decisions, you must require data-supported consultation. Break the habit of consultation based on unsupported/unsubstantiated traditions, hunches, and preferences:

- Request that official institutional data accompany consultation documents submitted for consideration.
- Support ongoing education and training about data governance and the use of data analytics to assist data-supported consultation.
- Require Faculty Senate, Staff Senate, and SGA surveys to be certified by the chief data or information officer to ensure that official data security and confidentiality protocols are followed.

For more on DSDM, refer to Section 5.1.

Budget Requests

All campuses have a university budget committee (UBC) in some form. In most cases, these committees are advisory to the president and are often chaired by the CFO. They function best when their role—and the role of subcommittees—in the consultation process is clearly defined, in writing. To nudge members to consider a broader institutional view and disrupt the development of a "beat others to the trough" mentality, it can be useful to require UBC members to submit written consultation documents that consider more than allocation increases for their own units. Consultation documents should include efficiency plans and resource reallocation plans that align with key performance indicators and strategic goals. Ongoing education/training regarding budget and finance-related matters will help members of the UBC understand and be able to convey the following concepts to their constituency groups:

- The relationship of *enrollment* to *budget* (e.g., the break-even point, retention, and student mix—full time, part time, in-state, out-of-state, grad, undergrad)
- ROI/value added

Refer to Section 2.2 for more discussion of budgets and resource allocation.

Personnel

Academic personnel considerations are a clearly defined area of consultation for faculty (see Section 3.3); decisions regarding faculty hiring, rank, and tenure require their written input. When joining a new institution, it is important to thoroughly understand faculty personnel policies and the role you play in hiring, rank, tenure, and separation, and in appeals regarding the aforementioned. If you find yourself in the position where you need to override faculty recommendations, go slowly and be sure to consult with them, following all current procedures and policies.

When new hires—whether faculty or staff—need to take place, be clear about the process for requesting and granting the filling of existing positions or the allocation of new ones. Make sure everyone is clear about your position as the hiring authority (and if not you, they need to be clear on who *is*) and what that means in terms of process. Inform units in advance that the data needed for requests should be quantitative, not 'mission' or qualitative data. Transparency in the position request process is created when all the 'asks' are shared among those who are asking. Help them to see all competing needs and give them the total budget to be allocated to fund all requests. For example, when the time came to consider the allocation of new faculty positions, one of us would work with her department chairs to get their requests and she would submit a prioritized list, ranked from highest need to lowest need, to the provost's office. Sharing these rankings with her department chairs ensured that the process was transparent and that all parties were aware of which new positions were higher priorities, and why.

Accreditations

The importance and purpose of institutional accreditation was emphasized in Section 5.3; it means the difference between eligibility and ineligibility for federal funding. Consultation plays an important role in the preparation of the self-study document that is reviewed by the evaluation team and the regional accreditation commission. Broad input and official institutional data are critical to developing a comprehensive self-study that adequately addresses accreditation standards. Although every effort should be made to seek feedback from a variety of stakeholder groups, this is *not* the time to air dirty laundry. We have both experienced numerous situations in which disgruntled faculty and staff attempted to use the accreditation team visit as an opportunity to embarrass and report campus leaders for perceived offenses, generally complaining of the lack of shared governance. People who engage in such behavior are unaware of the serious repercussions of sabotaging institutional accreditation. As a leader, it is your role to help faculty and staff understand its seriousness. Additionally, while it is their report, you will want to gently guide how these sections of the report are written.

One final point needs to be made regarding the self-study document for regional accreditation. Indisputably, the best self-study reports involve scores of people gathering data, writing subsections, and formatting and editing. As CEO, however, the president signs the document and thus bears total responsibility for its contents. Although it is rare that the president requires the self-study committee to completely overhaul the document to address insufficient responses to standards before agreeing to affix their signature, the president *is* empowered to make such a request to protect the institution from potential loss of accreditation or probation.

Later in this section, you can explore these ideas further in three case studies:

- The Case of the Secret Survey
- The Case of the Defeated Department (Parts A and B)
- The Case of the Accreditation Ambush

MICROCONTEXT

1	How much is data used during consultation and about what?

2 | Describe the role of the university budget committee:

3 | How are personnel positions currently requested?

SECTION FIVE: ESSENTIALS OF SHARED GOVERNANCE

SELF-REFLECTION

What do you know or need to know about your regional accreditation process?

ROADMAP 5.4
First: √ Assess what your team knows about finance and budgeting—and establish training and updates for your unit. Then:
If you have identified gaps while completing the microcontext (above), develop: a) A *consultation documentation process*—make sure to: - Require written consultation documents that consider more than allocation increases for their units. - Require the inclusion of efficiency plans and resource reallocation plans that align with key performance indicators and strategic goals.

Section Five: Essentials of Shared Governance

b) A *written process for requesting positions*:

Case Studies

1. THE CASE OF THE SECRET SURVEY

Dr. Dissatisfied thinks that there is no "real" shared governance in the division of academic affairs and that Abby Monkson, Faculty Senate president, along with the provost and all the deans, must be removed. Dr. Dissatisfied and two of the fifty faculty senators meet with Abby and say that they will call for a vote of no confidence on Abby at the next Faculty Senate meeting. Shaken, Abby inquires about and listens to their concerns and promises to do what it takes to give Dr. Dissatisfied and the two faculty senators more decision-making power in academic affairs.

They all meet again the next day and Dr. Dissatisfied strongly recommends that Abby, as Faculty Senate president, email a survey to all faculty members rating the provost and each dean on adherence to "real" shared governance. Dr. Dissatisfied tells Abby that they have already developed the survey using a free survey tool found on the internet; therefore, the survey can go out using the Faculty Senate email account before the end of the day.

The next morning, the campus is abuzz with talk of the survey. The 48 faculty senators who did not know about or attend Dr. Dissatisfied's meetings with Abby are angry that a survey was launched without their knowledge or consent. The chair of the Computer Science department comments that the free survey tool that was used does not adhere to university data security and confidentiality protocols. Someone forwards the survey to several students, and the students create a game to see how many times they can open and answer the survey before they are shut out.

Undaunted by the comments heard about the botched implementation, Dr. Dissatisfied—and a reluctant Abby—insist on meeting with Provost Earnest and the deans to discuss the survey results and make their demands.

> CONSIDER:
>
> Should Provost Earnest take the meeting? If so, how should the provost approach the meeting? If not, what and how should the provost communicate to Dr. Dissatisfied, Abby, and the division?

SECTION FIVE: ESSENTIALS OF SHARED GOVERNANCE

What genders and ethnicities did you imagine about these characters? (How) do any of your answers change based on their intersectional genders and ethnicities, in relation to other characters?

2A. THE CASE OF THE DEFEATED DEPARTMENT—PART A

The Cultural Studies department members were delighted to be awarded a tenure-track position to bring their faculty cohort to four full-time faculty. After a national search, the search and screen committee members were pleased to present their candidate of choice to Dean Wink. Out of four finalists, they recommended an internal candidate, Murphy Meager, to Dean Wink. They noted that although they didn't agree with this recommendation, the department vote as a whole (which included all full- and part-time faculty) chose Meager, who was currently serving as an adjunct in the department. Dean Wink had met all the candidates, and thought Meager was not qualified, and would have ranked them fourth. Further, Dean Wink is curious about the representation from the search committee that they don't think Meager is the best, but the full department does. Dean Wink holds the final authority about who is hired.

> CONSIDER:
>
> To reach a decision, what information does Dean Wink need, and from whom? If Dean Wink decides not to offer the position to Meager, what communication is needed and to whom? What potential pitfalls does Dean Wink need to be prepared to address/manage?

What genders and ethnicities did you imagine about these characters? (How) do any of your answers change based on their intersectional genders and ethnicities, in relation to other characters?

2B. THE CASE OF THE DEFEATED DEPARTMENT—PART B

Dean Wink met with the entire department, who provided no further evidence of how Meager might rank over the other three candidates—or even be qualified. Wink was able to get the department to rank the other three and let them know they would be offering the position to the next candidate in line. The department mounted a campaign to hire Meager, involving students who showed up at a Faculty Senate meeting, exclaiming, "We know that Meager might not be qualified, but we want them hired anyway." Dean Wink does not consider Meager to be qualified and plans to offer the position to one of the other three, using the ranking begrudgingly provided by the department.

CONSIDER:

What can Dean Wink do or say to the students or to faculty colleagues, within the ethics of best hiring practices? Is there anything that HR Director Mona Volador might need to do about the department faculty's behaviors? What concerns might Dean Wink have about the new hire and their entry into the department, and how might the dean deal with those?

What genders and ethnicities did you imagine about these characters? (How) do any of your answers change based on their intersectional genders and ethnicities, in relation to other characters?

3. The Case of the Accreditation Ambush

The university is engaged in its decennial regional re-accreditation process and things appear to be going swimmingly. A fifty-person self-study team consisting of faculty, staff, students, and administrators works together to develop a comprehensive self-study document addressing the 12 accreditation standards with accompanying institutional data. Pleased with the high level of cooperation and the high quality of the self-study report, President Petry sends a campus-wide email a week before the site visit to thank everyone for their hard work and cooperation and to share that the pre-visit feedback from the evaluation team is extremely positive.

Dr. Dogma refused to serve on the campus self-study team in order to reinforce their stance of opposing assessment of student learning using anything other than class grades. Dr. Dogma considers themself the 'moral compass' of the campus and believes that they are the only thing standing between the university and a downward slide into an ethical abyss. President Petry's email provokes Dr. Dogma's ire. They feel compelled to balance the self-study team's report with their own state-of-the-university report—a document that includes no mention of the 12 accreditation standards and is lacking in official institutional data.

Unbeknownst to President Petry, Dr. Dogma emails the evaluation team chair to request a private meeting during the site visit. The evaluation team chair writes back, agreeing to the meeting, and Dr. Dogma invites a few like-minded faculty members to join them. The evaluation team chair notifies the president that they have agreed to a meeting with Dr. Dogma. The president calls an emergency cabinet meeting to get advice on the best course of action, given that Dr. Dogma has been granted a meeting with the evaluation team chair. Provost Earnest receives a clandestinely obtained copy of Dr. Dogma's document from a faculty member who worked on the self-study team. The provost makes copies and takes them to the cabinet meeting.

CONSIDER:

How should President Petry handle the situation?

What genders and ethnicities did you imagine about these characters? (How) do any of your answers change based on their intersectional genders and ethnicities, in relation to other characters?

SECTION SIX: OPERATING ESSENTIALS

1. Updating Communication Strategies, Including Crisis Management Plans and Transparency
2. Review of Policies and Practices
3. Setting the Stage for Your Legacy

Higher education is a very people-intensive business, with multiple constituencies with different perspectives and priorities. Therefore, an understanding of the productive use of basic operating functions, such as communications and policies, is a must. Section Six opens by exploring how skillful communication with all stakeholder groups will play a role in your ability to accomplish your goals, then continues by delving into which policies and practices help or hinder goal attainment, how to handle conflicting policies, and how to track policy changes. This section comes full circle by revisiting the topic of your legacy—how that legacy is open to different interpretations by each stakeholder group and is context-dependent. Finally, Section Six closes with guidance on how to remain focused on the long-term health of the unit/institution throughout your tenure.

6.1. Updating Communication Strategies, Including Crisis Management Plans and Transparency

"The single biggest problem in communication is the illusion that it has taken place."
—*attributed to George Bernard Shaw and William H. Whyte*

KEY CONCEPTS AND CONSIDERATIONS

- Establish omnidirectional communication for all stakeholder groups.
- Crisis communication plans should be established for all units.
- Practice radical transparency.

Omnidirectional Communication for all Stakeholder Groups

Given that higher education is a very people-intensive business with multiple constituencies, the communication plan that you develop for your unit must make it possible not only for you to get your message across, but for others to communicate with you and each other. This means that your communication plan should include multiple communication channels and methods across different audiences. The greater your external constituency, the more planful your communication plan needs to be. If your communication is mostly internal, you will still want to consider carefully the best modalities and frequency of communication about various issues.

Keep in mind that students, faculty, staff, alumni, board members, and other stakeholders are multigenerational audiences with different communication preferences. This means your plan should include social media, print media, emails, text messages, and in some instances, radio and television, as well as virtual meetings and face-to-face meetings, when safe to do so. Skillful communication with all stakeholder groups will play a key role in your ability to accomplish your goals.

Work in concert with your institution's communication office to develop a plan that complements theirs and takes advantage of their planning resources, such as market testing of messages and branded materials.

Other things to take into consideration include:

- Achieving clarity about who is authorized to communicate through traditional and social media outlets on behalf of your unit to both internal and external audiences.

- Establishing a process for clearing or authorizing messages before public release.

- Ongoing evaluation of effectiveness and updating of the plan.

- Making provisions for resolving issues of free speech. For example, consider a case in which an employee uses a personal social media account or sends a campus email to denigrate the character of a coworker, or makes statements that discredit the university.

One thing you should never forget about communication is that every stakeholder group—and every individual—is listening to what you say, both verbally and written, from a different perspective. These stakeholders can hear or read the same message very differently. Therefore, it is best to keep your messaging as simple as possible and repeat important information as often as possible. When it comes to communicating broadly, concision and repetition are your friends. Major ideas that involve change will need to be repeated often, and in various modalities.

Crisis Communication Plan

The development of a crisis communication plan can seem like a waste of time—until it is needed. Weather events, active shooters, and power failures are but a few reasons why these plans are important in order to safeguard students, employees, and capital resources during a crisis. One of us was at an institution when armed police came to campus in response to a student with a gun. No crisis communication plan was followed, and that resulted in weeks of communication with parents, neighbors, students, and employees to correct misinformation fueled by fear. Crisis communication plans should be developed for all units, and they should be synchronized with the university's crisis plan. It is prudent to review and update these plans on a regular basis, and tabletop exercises should be used to test crisis communication plans under different scenarios. Ask that you or someone on your team be invited to the university's tabletop exercises to include your unit's perspective and response to emergencies and crises.[5]

Critical Questions for Crisis Communication Planning

1. Who is 'in charge' and who has which roles?
2. What relationships need to be established prior to a crisis (e.g., local law enforcement)?
3. What types of practice are needed prior to an actual crisis (e.g., tabletop exercises)?
4. How will you ensure the safety of students, faculty, and staff?
5. How will you communicate with your team during a crisis? What modality(ies) will be used?
6. How will you prevent or minimize the loss of key resources such as facilities, IT infrastructure, lab samples and data?

Radical Transparency

The last communication topic, but arguably the most important, is *radical transparency*—a communication approach that involves sharing as much information and data as possible with as many stakeholders as possible to increase openness and understanding within an organization.

Ideally, there is transparency at every level of an organization, but unfortunately, this is not always the case. It is more likely that most communication comes from cabinet-level officers. Academic and administrative departments rarely make an effort to be completely transparent, while requesting greater transparency from upper administration. They are likely to define transparency as being allowed *access* to all information, but not as sharing much information.

If your campus does not practice radical transparency, you should be the first leader to try it. Make sure that you publicly and broadly share your unit's goals, inputs, performance outcomes, and annual reports on a regular basis.

---

[5] You can find key resources for crisis communication planning through Ready.gov and NACUBO. Ready.gov is a federally sponsored website that contains resources to aid individuals, families, and organizations to prepare for, respond to, and minimize the negative impacts of emergencies. The site includes a section called *Ready Campus*, which provides higher education institutions guidance on planning, responding to, and recovering from natural or man-made disasters, including acts of violence such as active shooters. The National Association of College and University Business Officers' website (www.nacubo.org) also offers resources to aid colleges and universities with emergency and disaster preparedness and recovery.

Of course, this needs to be done within performance confidentiality policies and within legal limits. Practicing radical transparency may feel risky because not only will you publicly share your victories, but also your defeats. This may seem particularly uncomfortable during times of budget cuts and layoffs, at a time when many people want to "keep their heads down" and hope they or their unit are left untouched. However, the willingness to practice radical transparency consistently is not only in keeping with the spirit of shared governance, it also creates an opportunity for organizational learning by empowering you to work through issues with your team and other stakeholders—a step that can help move you past fearing the worst, allow you to refocus your energy on continuous improvement, and can win you the respect of well-intentioned members of the campus community. Radical transparency also allows peers to learn from each other as they share best practices and to avoid repeating the same mistakes.

Later in this section, you can explore these ideas further in this case study:

- The Case of the Bill(Board)

MICROCONTEXT

1	What communications plans exist on campus?

Section Six: Operating Essentials

2 | How are the plans used?

3 | Are there mechanisms in place for omnidirectional communication for all stakeholder groups?

4 | Are there multiple communication channels for different audiences? List the audiences and communication channels used for each:

Section Six: Operating Essentials

5	Is it clear who is authorized to communicate through traditional and social media outlets on behalf of the university/unit?
6	How are official messages cleared/authorized before being released to the public?
7	Is the effectiveness of campus-wide and unit-wide communication assessed? How often?

8	If an employee uses a personal social media account or sends a campus email to denigrate the character of a coworker or makes statements that discredit the university, does your communication plan address these types of situations?
9	Does your unit have a crisis communication plan?
10	Is your unit's crisis communication plan synchronized with the university's crisis communication plan?

Section Six: Operating Essentials

| 11 | How often do you review your crisis communication plan and update it with your team? |

| 12 | Does the university conduct tabletop exercises to test crisis communication plans under different scenarios? |

| 13 | Are you or someone on your team invited to the university's tabletop exercises to include your unit's perspective and response to emergencies and crises? |

14	Does your campus practice radical transparency at all levels of the institution? Are goals, inputs, performance outcomes, and annual reports for all units shared publicly, and are they easily accessible?
15	Does your campus have easily accessible, publicly displayed dashboards, institutional research website and reports, and unit websites and reports?

SELF-REFLECTION

What is your comfort level with different communication modalities? Which modalities do you need to learn? For which do you need to increase your level of comfort?

In Section 5.1, you reflected on your comfort level with sharing data. As you take it to a level of radical transparency, do any of your answers change?

Case Studies

1. THE CASE OF THE BILL(BOARD)

Newby Nelson is pleased to have an increase in the annual budget for media buys to attract and track potential students. Newby hires a firm that uses data analytics to determine the most effective messages and placements across various social media platforms. At the Board of Trustees meeting, Newby is pleased to report about the process and about a modest increase in the anticipated incoming class. Newby is expecting the board members to be pleased and is surprised when the conversation quickly turns into a critique about the lack of the institution's presence on local billboards. Unbeknownst to Newby, Big Buck Bentley's cousin owns the local billboard company.

CONSIDER:

What might be influencing this disconnect? How might Newby deal with the Trustees' concerns, since Newby knows that billboards have low return on investment to attract potential students?

What genders and ethnicities did you imagine about these characters? (How) do any of your answers change based on their intersectional genders and ethnicities, in relation to other characters?

6.2. Review of Policies and Practices

> *"Only three things happen naturally in organizations: friction, confusion, and underperformance. Everything else requires leadership."* —Peter Drucker

> KEY CONCEPTS AND CONSIDERATIONS
>
> - Determine which policies and practices help or hinder goal attainment.

Dealing with Outlier Policies

Among the things you will inherit when the leadership baton is passed to you is a set of pre-existing policies created by past administrations for a particular set of circumstances at a particular point in time. Sometimes those policies are too restrictive, created to deal with an outlier situation—such as a rogue faculty or staff—rather than keeping in mind the entire institution. One of us worked at an institution that actually referred to a policy as "the [insert name of rogue employee] rule."

When you step into your role, you will be expected to achieve results that may or may not be enabled by the policies and practices in place. It is up to you, as an incoming leader, to review policies, considering the function of your unit, your goals and objectives, human and financial resources, and the external operating environment. Don't be afraid to question outlier policies (those that are out of step with best practices in higher ed), and don't be afraid to ask to change policies. If you did not review your institution's policies before you took the job, ask for a copy before or soon after arriving on campus. Otherwise, you may default to operating under the policies of your previous institution. This is one of the more frequent mistakes made by new senior leaders.

Auditing Existing Policies

Inquire about the last time policies were audited for alignment with your unit's goals and objectives. Keep in mind that your policies may need to change as your unit's goals and objectives change. Get an understanding of the process to update, create, or eliminate policies, and the role of shared governance in that process. Make sure policy changes are tracked, documented, and communicated clearly to all stakeholders. If you are responsible for a relatively new unit, or an existing unit with new responsibilities and expectations, or if the conditions in the external operating environment that impact your unit have changed drastically, conduct your own policy audit to determine if existing policies help or hinder you from achieving your unit's goals.

Reviewing, auditing, and updating policies can be arduous and should not be tackled alone. Create a task force of 3-5 people to help you conduct the review. Once the review is complete, keep policies current by reviewing them on a regular basis. Policy review is a task that can be assigned to one of your staff members and can be an annual agenda item at your staff meetings.

Another thing you want to look out for are policy conflicts. Your unit's policies should align with related federal, state, local, and, if applicable, system policies. Occasionally, there will be conflicts between your unit's policies and the policies of other units. Several years ago, one of us encountered a situation where two VPs' policies on the same topic were in conflict. These two VPs stayed at loggerheads with each other; their feud was the stuff of legends. They despised working together—until they realized that they were both operating on current and approved university policies that hindered each other's operations. After this was discovered, they were able to sit down and review the situation, write a new policy that suited the needs of both units, and obtain improved outcomes for both units. The point of this story is to never assume that current and approved policies are consistent from unit to unit. When you assume an administrative position, compare your unit's policies to those of the units that you depend on or those that depend on you. This situation also emphasizes the need for a unified and coordinated policy approval and tracking system.

Reviewing Practices

Finally, don't be surprised if you discover that your team's practices do not match written campus policies. This can occur for at least a couple of reasons. The unit may have had a long-serving leader, or may have long-serving team members, who remember and still operate from old policies. Conversely, lots of turnover in leadership and in staff and faculty can also result in a lack of congruence between policy and day-to-day practices. In the former situation, work with your team members during your one-on-one meetings to move them away from outdated practices. In the latter, it is easier to address the issue as a group if most team members are relatively new. In both cases, remind your team that policies are legally binding and that all employees are responsible for knowing and following the most current policies.

Later in this section, you can explore these ideas further in these two case studies:

- The Case of the Southpaw Seeking Assistance (or The Case of the Retired Redbird)
- The Case of the Curveballs, Sliders, and Sinkers

SECTION SIX: OPERATING ESSENTIALS

MICROCONTEXT

| 1 | What policies need revision at your current institution? |

| 2 | Are there policies that help or hinder you from achieving your unit's goals? |

Polices that help: *Policies that hinder:*

3	How is policy used to enhance or stall change?
4	Are policies and practices reviewed and updated on a regular basis?
5	Is there an agreed-upon process for changes to policy and practice? If so, what is the process to update, create, or eliminate policies?

Section Six: Operating Essentials

6 | What is the role of shared governance in this process?

7 | How are policy changes tracked, documented, and communicated clearly to all stakeholders?

8 | Are policies consistent from unit to unit, or are there policy conflicts between/among units?

SELF-REFLECTION
Policy work can be very tedious and detailed. How suitable are you for writing, reviewing, and updating policies?

Section Six: Operating Essentials

ROADMAP 6.2

Take these critical steps:

√ Review policies in light of the function of your unit, your goals and objectives, human and financial resources, and the external operating environment.

√ Review policies before taking a job or soon after arriving on campus. Otherwise, you may default to operating under the policies of your previous institution.

√ Inquire about the last time policies were audited for alignment with your unit's goals and objectives.

Then:

Develop a plan for adding or revising policies, as needed:

Case Studies

1. THE CASE OF THE SOUTHPAW SEEKING ASSISTANCE (OR THE CASE OF THE RETIRED REDBIRD)

Newby Nelson, the new vice president of enrollment management and student affairs, is approached by Coach Southpaw Sanders, a former pitcher for the St. Louis Cardinals. Southpaw is seeking assistance with recruiting more student-athletes for the baseball team. Newby was not involved in the recruitment of student-athletes at their former institution and has no prior experience to draw from.

> CONSIDER:
>
> What policies should Newby review before helping Southpaw recruit more student-athletes? If policies need updating or if new policies need to be written, who should shepherd and champion the polices? Newby, Southpaw, or both? What are the issues to consider?
>
> What genders and ethnicities did you imagine about these characters? (How) do any of your answers change based on their intersectional genders and ethnicities, in relation to other characters?

SECTION SIX: OPERATING ESSENTIALS

2. THE CASE OF THE CURVEBALLS, SLIDERS, AND SINKERS

Baseball coach Southpaw Sanders has been promoted to athletic director upon the retirement of AD Duncan, a likeable, easygoing person who held the position previously for 15 years. The newly appointed AD Sanders has performed admirably as a coach and is well-connected and nationally known, due to their record-breaking performance as a pitcher for the St. Louis Cardinals. Sanders has laid out an exciting vision for JRU's athletic program and has promised the president that they would raise all standards related to their department.

Despite Southpaw's vision and experience, some members of the athletics department are a little concerned about the new AD's by-the-book approach to operations, as it is a departure from the informal style of the former AD. The assistant AD for academic advising in the department, Max Myway, has decided not to sweat the change in leadership and intends to carry on with business as usual. From Max's perspective, professionals should be able to basically do as they please as long as required tasks are performed.

Two months into Southpaw's tenure as AD, Max disappears for 6 work days with no notice, no contact left with the office, and no approved leave form. Upon returning, Max seeks out Southpaw, who is in the gym, just to let the AD know that they disappear from time to time to care for their aging parents, who live 500 miles away. Max also explains that AD Duncan never had a problem with this unannounced time away from the office. Observing the puzzled look on Southpaw's face, Max says, "What's the problem? I cleared my desk of all assignments before I left, and student-athletes can always reach me via email or text." Max's attitude and comments enrage Southpaw, and the AD reprimands Max in the presence of several student-athletes and staff members who are gathering in the gym for practice. In addition to Max's disappearance, the assistant AD had held an unapproved pool party for their teenage son and 20 guests in the aquatics center, for which Max had received a letter of reprimand. Southpaw has had their fill of Max and decides to demote them.

Furious about the demotion and embarrassed about the public reprimand, Max sends a scathing email to the department and all student-athletes, stating that they will no longer subject themselves to the tyrannical leadership of AD Sanders and that they will, henceforth, be working remotely while caring for their parents. The email is filled with baseball analogies and metaphors and goes on to excoriate Southpaw by stating that the AD has created a hostile work environment by throwing the curveballs, sinkers, and sliders Southpaw was famous for when they were a starting pitcher for the Cardinals. The email ends by resurrecting an old rumor accusing Southpaw of using illegal performance-enhancing drugs when they were a pro baseball player and alleges that Southpaw's stats are fraudulent and that, therefore, Southpaw should be disqualified for induction at Cooperstown.

Max works remotely for two weeks until a few colleagues gently suggest that they come back, apologize, and try to cooperate for the sake of the student-athletes. Max heeds this advice and files for FMLA after returning to work to cover their 6-day disappearance. Max refuses to apologize, however. A few days later, Max receives a certified letter from the HR director informing them of their termination. Max immediately contacts an attorney to file a lawsuit for a hostile work environment and wrongful termination. The university, Southpaw, and the HR director are named in the suit. Likewise, Southpaw sues Max for defamation.

CONSIDER:

What valid evidence, if any, does Max have for their claims? What valid evidence, if any, does Southpaw have for their claim?

What genders and ethnicities did you imagine about these characters? (How) do any of your answers change based on their intersectional genders and ethnicities, in relation to other characters?

6.3. Setting the Stage for Your Legacy (Revisited)

"Put aside your pride, set down your arrogance, and remember your grave." —*Ali ibn Abi Talib*

> **KEY CONCEPTS AND CONSIDERATIONS**
>
> - Your legacy is open to interpretation by others and is context-dependent.
> - Focus on the long-term health of the institution/unit.

Overview

Now, we return to the topic of legacy. In our initial discussion of legacy in Section One, we explained that the "sprint relay" leadership model is based on the idea of the decreasing tenure of senior leaders in higher education. This model also acknowledges the difficulties and constraints created by significant challenges in the macro environment and the micro environment. Given these factors, how do you create a meaningful and realistic legacy?

First, keep in mind that your legacy is open to interpretation by others and is context-dependent. As mentioned earlier, senior leaders are in a double bind created by the divergent expectations of internal and external stakeholders. Each group will interpret your legacy based on their perception of how much time you spent directly engaging them and their issues, relative to other constituency groups. Your legacy will also be judged according to the relative financial state of the institution. Also, the same people who complained about you while you were in your role, may praise you when they compare you to subsequent leaders who are at the helm during more difficult financial times.

Ultimately, you cannot control how you will be remembered as a leader; therefore, one point cannot be emphasized enough:

Focus on the long-term health of the institution/unit.

It's not sexy, but it gets the job done. Are there projects that may not be glamorous or high-profile but that must be successfully completed so that your unit or institution can make progress? Get busy working on them. Your actions may not have the *wow* factor that garners hundreds of likes on social media, but if your work sets the university up for the next level of success, do it anyway—even if it is your successor who gets to cross the finish line and take credit for the ultimate win.

Finally, whether or not others remember your role in creating meaningful and positive change, *you* will know. One of us created two new units on campus within months of being in that senior leadership role: a center for teaching and learning, and a new DEI office. This work included hiring a CDO, as well as elevating DEI visibility in consequential ways. Today, she often hears about the CDO's great work, but her own role is largely invisible. Also, the center for teaching and learning played a crucial role in faculty development regarding changes to teaching modalities during the COVID pandemic. No one remembers that the center did not exist prior to her creation of it. Laying the foundation in both of these areas positioned the institution to be able to respond more effectively to a changing landscape. Her legacy, even if not visible, is still meaningful.

You can never really predict how long you will be in a leadership position. Any number of things, personal and professional, will help determine the length of your tenure. Additionally, you can't accurately predict how others will perceive what you have done, after you have finished your leg of the race. Therefore, our advice to you is to focus on long-term institutional health, and on your own mental, emotional, and physical health. Keep in mind that there is life after leadership, and you want to be as healthy as possible to enjoy it. And finally, your legacy will most likely be one you can be proud of if, as we stated in the beginning, you shift your perspective from just getting and keeping a job, to doing your job with integrity.

Later in this section, you can explore these ideas further in this case study:

- The Case of the Pensive President

SECTION SIX: OPERATING ESSENTIALS

MICROCONTEXT

1	Given fiscal and human resources, inherited challenges, and the external operating environment, what are realistic stretch goals for the institution/unit that can be accomplished in 3-5 years?
2	From the list of realistic stretch goals that can be accomplished in 3-5 years, what is the *one goal* that, if accomplished, will result in the long-term health of the institution/unit?
3	Are there projects that may not be glamorous or high-profile but that must be completed successfully so that your unit/institution can make progress?

SELF-REFLECTION
What do you hope is your legacy for your current position?
What are you doing to create it?

Section Six: Operating Essentials

ROADMAP 6.3

This entire workbook is designed to provide you with the roadmap for a successful experience, leading to your legacy. While counterintuitive, there is no roadmap to complete for Section 6.3. However, the entirety of Section Seven, in the following pages, will help you to create the steps that will allow you to narrow your focus for your legacy endeavors. So, take a deep breath as you move on to the final section: "Pulling it All Together."

Case Studies

1. THE CASE OF THE PENSIVE PRESIDENT

President Petry is in a pensive mood and is reviewing the list of goals developed in year one of their presidency. Feeling tired and overwhelmed—especially since the advent of the pandemic and the concomitant enrollment downturn—the president decides to finally rank order the goals, a task that never made it on their first-year to-do list. Given the state of the world and with two years remaining on a five-year contract, the president wants to spend the remaining time focused on the top three goals.

> CONSIDER:
>
> Given your own approach to higher-ed leadership and what you know from the previous case studies of Jackson Rockgrove University, rank the following goals in terms of most likely or least likely to positively impact the long-term health of the institution.
>
> _____ Establish a center for faculty development
>
> _____ Conduct a fundraising campaign for an alumni walk of fame
>
> _____ Reduce deferred maintenance by 10%
>
> _____ Break ground on a new performing arts building
>
> _____ Rebrand the institution, including a redesigned logo and new slogan
>
> _____ Become a test-optional or test-blind campus
>
> _____ Establish a research foundation
>
> _____ Expand the athletics program
>
> _____ Restructure academic affairs

Section Six: Operating Essentials

Explain your rankings:

SECTION SEVEN: PULLING IT ALL TOGETHER

Running the Race

> **KEY CONCEPTS AND CONSIDERATIONS**
>
> - Inherited issues determine a lot of what you can and can't do.
> - You need to plan on a short timeframe.
> - You have a limited ability to create meaningful change.
> - Beware of hubris.
> - Success is possible if you are well-informed and take courageous actions.
> - In this workbook, we have only covered the highlights of each area. *All* of these topics are more complex and nuanced.

Looking over your Self-Reflections and your answers to the Roadmap questions throughout Sections One through Six, it's time to develop *your* Roadmap for the first few months (not more than six!) in your new leadership role. You have diagnosed the issues—an important step. Now, as you build this roadmap of activities to do, data to collect, and communication strategies to implement, you will want to decide the priority order. It is probable that you will list more than is possible to do; therefore, ranking priorities is as important as the activities themselves.

SECTION SEVEN: PULLING IT ALL TOGETHER

SELF-REFLECTION

In what ways do you need to shift your perspective to think of leadership as a relay?

What else do you need/want to know in order to be well-informed about successful, sprint-relay leadership in this new reality?

What parts of this sprint-relay paradigm resonate for you?

What parts of this sprint-relay paradigm may not apply to you?

Your 3-6 Month Roadmap

Build your individualized strategic plan, drawing from the material you have already provided in response to the Roadmap questions in Sections One through Six of this book. As you revisit each roadmap, first consider the macro context in higher education. You may wish to consider technology, politics, demographics, and aspects of the external operating environment. If your institution is part of a state system, what is the current climate for the system that creates a macro context for your institution?

Then, for each action item on the roadmap, take a few moments to consider the following:

1. **What do I hope to achieve by this activity? What is/are my outcome(s)?** It's worth spending some time answering this question, as your answer will help you when you are creating a priority list and/or a timeline for all the work to be done. Remember, the time will move quickly, and your list will likely be much longer than is possible to accomplish in 3-6 months. While some items may be able to be delayed, many are time-sensitive. Once you are 'established,' some may no longer be salient to helping you succeed.

2. **Identify the specific strategies or activities needed to complete this action item.** This is where you clarify *what* you need to do.

3. **Identify any data you need to collect.** This is part of the *how* you will get this done. What quantitative data might you need? What qualitative data, such as background information, might you need?

4. **Who do you need to involve?** Clarify *who* you need to work with.

5. **What is your plan for communicating this step transparently?** This is the other part of *how*—what communication strategies will you use? What modalities will you use? What data is important to share, and how will you share it?

6. **What is the timeline?** Clarify *when* this needs to happen. The timeline can be a rough estimate by month, or if possible, by week. For example, what do you want to do in week one? In week six?

7. **Finally, look over your list and rank the items in priority order.** Use your outcomes and timeline to help you determine what is both possible and a priority. It's okay to delete some items that don't rise to the top. You can also push some to year two or three—but be realistic. By then, the macro and micro contexts will probably have changed enough that you will need to revise those items, evaluating them for relevance first.

Roadmap 1.1—Your Relay Leg (page 11)

Identify strategies to overcome any resistance to ideas that might ultimately benefit your success in this leadership role.

OUTCOME:

STRATEGIES / ACTIVITIES:

DATA NEEDED:

Section Seven: Pulling it All Together

WHOM TO INVOLVE:

COMMUNICATION NEEDED (BETTER MODALITIES):

WHEN (TIMING: SPECIFIC WEEK/MONTH):

PRIORITY RANKING:

Roadmap 1.2—Inheritance (page 22)

Checklist—Items to Do First:

√ Assemble qualitative and quantitative data needed to review performance of direct reports, faculty, and staff.

Develop *(a)* a list of your performance expectations for your team...

LIST OF PERFORMANCE EXPECTATIONS:

...and *(b)* strategies to communicate these performance expectations effectively:

OUTCOME:

STRATEGIES / ACTIVITIES:

Section Seven: Pulling it All Together

DATA NEEDED:

WHOM TO INVOLVE:

COMMUNICATION NEEDED (BETTER MODALITIES):

WHEN (TIMING: SPECIFIC WEEK/MONTH):

PRIORITY RANKING:

1.2 CONTINUED. Prioritize and develop strategies for inherited personnel issues, including timeline for completion, and responsibly delegate.

OUTCOME:

STRATEGIES / ACTIVITIES:

DATA NEEDED:

Section Seven: Pulling it All Together

WHOM TO INVOLVE:

COMMUNICATION NEEDED (BETTER MODALITIES):

WHEN (TIMING: SPECIFIC WEEK/MONTH):

PRIORITY RANKING:

1.2 CONTINUED. Articulate your understanding and commitment to equity and inclusion.

OUTCOME:

STRATEGIES / ACTIVITIES:

DATA NEEDED:

Section Seven: Pulling it All Together

WHOM TO INVOLVE:

COMMUNICATION NEEDED (BETTER MODALITIES):

WHEN (TIMING: SPECIFIC WEEK/MONTH):

PRIORITY RANKING:

1.2 CONTINUED. List methods to communicate your expectations and commitment to equity/inclusion, and how you will reinforce them over time.

OUTCOME:

STRATEGIES / ACTIVITIES:

DATA NEEDED:

Section Seven: Pulling it All Together

WHOM TO INVOLVE:

COMMUNICATION NEEDED (BETTER MODALITIES):

WHEN (TIMING: SPECIFIC WEEK/MONTH):

PRIORITY RANKING:

1.2 CONTINUED. Delineate which policies/practices need revision first to help the institution (or your area) become more equitable/inclusive.

> OUTCOME:

> STRATEGIES / ACTIVITIES:

> DATA NEEDED:

Section Seven: Pulling it All Together

WHOM TO INVOLVE:

COMMUNICATION NEEDED (BETTER MODALITIES):

WHEN (TIMING: SPECIFIC WEEK/MONTH):

PRIORITY RANKING:

1.2 CONTINUED. Do you have a plan to uncover and address long-lived biases (sexism, racism and homophobia) as part of culture? Please describe or develop a rough outline.

OUTCOME:

STRATEGIES / ACTIVITIES:

DATA NEEDED:

Section Seven: Pulling It All Together

WHOM TO INVOLVE:

COMMUNICATION NEEDED (BETTER MODALITIES):

WHEN (TIMING: SPECIFIC WEEK/MONTH):

PRIORITY RANKING:

1.2 CONTINUED. Describe the plan to address any issues related to xenophobia.

OUTCOME:

STRATEGIES / ACTIVITIES:

DATA NEEDED:

Section Seven: Pulling it All Together

WHOM TO INVOLVE:

COMMUNICATION NEEDED (BETTER MODALITIES):

WHEN (TIMING: SPECIFIC WEEK/MONTH):

PRIORITY RANKING:

Roadmap 1.3—Your Legacy (page 35)

Develop and prioritize realistic stretch goals tied to vision and taking into consideration inherited issues.

OUTCOME:

STRATEGIES / ACTIVITIES:

DATA NEEDED:

Section Seven: Pulling it All Together

WHOM TO INVOLVE:

COMMUNICATION NEEDED (BETTER MODALITIES):

WHEN (TIMING: SPECIFIC WEEK/MONTH):

PRIORITY RANKING:

1.3 CONTINUED. Identify and schedule self-care activities.

OUTCOME:

STRATEGIES / ACTIVITIES:

DATA NEEDED:

Section Seven: Pulling it All Together

WHOM TO INVOLVE:

COMMUNICATION NEEDED (BETTER MODALITIES):

WHEN (TIMING: SPECIFIC WEEK/MONTH):

PRIORITY RANKING:

1.3 CONTINUED. Identify coaching and support groups for your leadership journey.

OUTCOME:

STRATEGIES / ACTIVITIES:

DATA NEEDED:

Section Seven: Pulling it All Together

WHOM TO INVOLVE:

COMMUNICATION NEEDED (BETTER MODALITIES):

WHEN (TIMING: SPECIFIC WEEK/MONTH):

PRIORITY RANKING:

ROADMAP 2.1—POWER DYNAMICS (PAGE 52)

Where are the places or events where you might observe informal relationships or power dynamics among people/constituents? What are your plans to create opportunities for observation?

OUTCOME:

STRATEGIES / ACTIVITIES:

DATA NEEDED:

Section Seven: Pulling it All Together

WHOM TO INVOLVE:

COMMUNICATION NEEDED (BETTER MODALITIES):

WHEN (TIMING: SPECIFIC WEEK/MONTH):

PRIORITY RANKING:

2.1 CONTINUED. Develop a plan to use Facebook and other social media to learn about people and relationships at the institution.

OUTCOME:

STRATEGIES / ACTIVITIES:

DATA NEEDED:

Section Seven: Pulling it All Together

WHOM TO INVOLVE:

COMMUNICATION NEEDED (BETTER MODALITIES):

WHEN (TIMING: SPECIFIC WEEK/MONTH):

PRIORITY RANKING:

Roadmap 2.2—Climate, Gossip, Campus Lore, and Misinformation (page 77)

Checklist—Items to Do First:

√ Read past minutes of shared governance bodies to help you discover the campus culture.

How are you going to learn the lived mission at the institution? Where will you look for clues?

OUTCOME:

STRATEGIES / ACTIVITIES:

DATA NEEDED:

Section Seven: Pulling it All Together

WHOM TO INVOLVE:

COMMUNICATION NEEDED (BETTER MODALITIES):

WHEN (TIMING: SPECIFIC WEEK/MONTH):

PRIORITY RANKING:

2.2 CONTINUED. If you know of any areas of misunderstanding at the institution, what data will you gather to correct them, and how will you communicate the findings?

OUTCOME:

STRATEGIES / ACTIVITIES:

DATA NEEDED:

Section Seven: Pulling it All Together

WHOM TO INVOLVE:

COMMUNICATION NEEDED (BETTER MODALITIES):

WHEN (TIMING: SPECIFIC WEEK/MONTH):

PRIORITY RANKING:

2.2 CONTINUED. What processes do you want to implement to set norms for your newly formed area?

OUTCOME:

STRATEGIES / ACTIVITIES:

DATA NEEDED:

Section Seven: Pulling it All Together

WHOM TO INVOLVE:

COMMUNICATION NEEDED (BETTER MODALITIES):

WHEN (TIMING: SPECIFIC WEEK/MONTH):

PRIORITY RANKING:

2.2 CONTINUED. Who will you talk to about power dynamics on campus to assess them? What's your plan? Include how you will identify opinion leaders, given the informal power they hold at the institution.

> OUTCOME:

> STRATEGIES / ACTIVITIES:

> DATA NEEDED:

Section Seven: Pulling it All Together

WHOM TO INVOLVE:

COMMUNICATION NEEDED (BETTER MODALITIES):

WHEN (TIMING: SPECIFIC WEEK/MONTH):

PRIORITY RANKING:

2.2 CONTINUED. List ways to uncover and address long-lived biases that have become part of the campus culture (sexism, racism, homophobia, xenophobia, etc.).

OUTCOME:

STRATEGIES / ACTIVITIES:

DATA NEEDED:

Section Seven: Pulling it All Together

WHOM TO INVOLVE:

COMMUNICATION NEEDED (BETTER MODALITIES):

WHEN (TIMING: SPECIFIC WEEK/MONTH):

PRIORITY RANKING:

2.2 CONTINUED. Examine patterns of hiring and/or people leaving the institution (e.g., look for lack of equity by race, sex, etc.), including an analysis of whether or not BIPOC leave in greater proportions. (If the institution is not hiring qualified BIPOC proportionately, uncover the reasons given by search committees/hiring managers.)

OUTCOME:

STRATEGIES / ACTIVITIES:

DATA NEEDED:

Section Seven: Pulling it All Together

WHOM TO INVOLVE:

COMMUNICATION NEEDED (BETTER MODALITIES):

WHEN (TIMING: SPECIFIC WEEK/MONTH):

PRIORITY RANKING:

2.2 CONTINUED. Does your institution/unit provide appropriate and adequate resources to support the success of students, faculty, and staff with differing abilities? If not, determine ways to address their needs.

OUTCOME:

STRATEGIES / ACTIVITIES:

DATA NEEDED:

Section Seven: Pulling it All Together

WHOM TO INVOLVE:

COMMUNICATION NEEDED (BETTER MODALITIES):

WHEN (TIMING: SPECIFIC WEEK/MONTH):

PRIORITY RANKING:

2.2 CONTINUED. If the data you gathered yields inequities, how will you begin to address them? What is the timeframe for these actions? What is realistic? What foundation needs to be laid first?

OUTCOME:

STRATEGIES / ACTIVITIES:

DATA NEEDED:

Section Seven: Pulling it All Together

WHOM TO INVOLVE:

COMMUNICATION NEEDED (BETTER MODALITIES):

WHEN (TIMING: SPECIFIC WEEK/MONTH):

PRIORITY RANKING:

Roadmap 2.3—Setting Boundaries (page 99)

What is your plan for getting to know colleagues more socially within your role?

OUTCOME:

STRATEGIES / ACTIVITIES:

DATA NEEDED:

Section Seven: Pulling it All Together

WHOM TO INVOLVE:

COMMUNICATION NEEDED (BETTER MODALITIES):

WHEN (TIMING: SPECIFIC WEEK/MONTH):

PRIORITY RANKING:

2.3 CONTINUED. If you promote others from within, how will you help them learn how to set boundaries?

OUTCOME:

STRATEGIES / ACTIVITIES:

DATA NEEDED:

Section Seven: Pulling it All Together

WHOM TO INVOLVE:

COMMUNICATION NEEDED (BETTER MODALITIES):

WHEN (TIMING: SPECIFIC WEEK/MONTH):

PRIORITY RANKING:

Roadmap 3.1—Building Internal and External Relationships (page 117)

List the important internal and external stakeholders in your current leadership position.

STAKEHOLDERS:

Who do you need to develop a relationship with horizontally?

OUTCOME:

STRATEGIES / ACTIVITIES:

Section Seven: Pulling it All Together

DATA NEEDED:

WHOM TO INVOLVE:

COMMUNICATION NEEDED (BETTER MODALITIES):

WHEN (TIMING: SPECIFIC WEEK/MONTH):

PRIORITY RANKING:

3.1 CONTINUED. Who do you need to develop a relationship with vertically?

OUTCOME:

STRATEGIES / ACTIVITIES:

DATA NEEDED:

Section Seven: Pulling it All Together

WHOM TO INVOLVE:

COMMUNICATION NEEDED (BETTER MODALITIES):

WHEN (TIMING: SPECIFIC WEEK/MONTH):

PRIORITY RANKING:

3.1 CONTINUED. List the meetings you need to conduct and how frequently.

MEETINGS (AND FREQUENCY):

How do you want to modify the current meetings to make them useful (and kept to a minimum)?

OUTCOME:

STRATEGIES / ACTIVITIES:

Section Seven: Pulling it All Together

DATA NEEDED:

WHOM TO INVOLVE:

COMMUNICATION NEEDED (BETTER MODALITIES):

WHEN (TIMING: SPECIFIC WEEK/MONTH):

PRIORITY RANKING:

3.1 CONTINUED. Think of quick and easy ways to build relationships via recognition.

OUTCOME:

STRATEGIES / ACTIVITIES:

DATA NEEDED:

Section Seven: Pulling It All Together

WHOM TO INVOLVE:

COMMUNICATION NEEDED (BETTER MODALITIES):

WHEN (TIMING: SPECIFIC WEEK/MONTH):

PRIORITY RANKING:

3.1 CONTINUED. Given the position of your institution in the community, what types of service do you need to do?

OUTCOME:

STRATEGIES / ACTIVITIES:

DATA NEEDED:

Section Seven: Pulling it All Together

WHOM TO INVOLVE:

COMMUNICATION NEEDED (BETTER MODALITIES):

WHEN (TIMING: SPECIFIC WEEK/MONTH):

PRIORITY RANKING:

3.1 CONTINUED. Are there local/state leadership boards you want to join (e.g., chamber, leadership of county/state/city, etc.)?

OUTCOME:

STRATEGIES / ACTIVITIES:

DATA NEEDED:

Section Seven: Pulling it All Together

WHOM TO INVOLVE:

COMMUNICATION NEEDED (BETTER MODALITIES):

WHEN (TIMING: SPECIFIC WEEK/MONTH):

PRIORITY RANKING:

3.1 CONTINUED. How might you connect with your peers through existing structures (or set one up)?

OUTCOME:

STRATEGIES / ACTIVITIES:

DATA NEEDED:

Section Seven: Pulling it All Together

WHOM TO INVOLVE:

COMMUNICATION NEEDED (BETTER MODALITIES):

WHEN (TIMING: SPECIFIC WEEK/MONTH):

PRIORITY RANKING:

ROADMAP 3.2—INFORMATION GATHERING AND DETERMINING WHO TO TRUST (PAGE 137)

CHECKLIST—ITEMS TO DO:

√ Make a list of the reports you need and get access to them.

√ Identify reports you need that are not generated. Working with the IR Office, develop these reports.

LIST OF REPORTS NEEDED:

Section Seven: Pulling it All Together

REPORTS NEEDED THAT AREN'T GENERATED (REPORTS THAT YOU'LL NEED TO DEVELOP WITH IR):

Now, decide how you want to use these reports, both existing and requested. Who do they need to be shared with, how, and when?

```
OUTCOME:



```

```
STRATEGIES / ACTIVITIES:




```

```
DATA NEEDED:



```

Section Seven: Pulling it All Together

WHOM TO INVOLVE:

COMMUNICATION NEEDED (BETTER MODALITIES):

WHEN (TIMING: SPECIFIC WEEK/MONTH):

PRIORITY RANKING:

Roadmap 3.3—Examining Shared Governance (page 156)

Checklist—Items to Do:

√ Review the AAUP Red Book or faculty or staff contract and handbooks.

√ Review past climate/satisfaction surveys or minutes of shared governance committees at your institution to get some sense of actual practices/attitudes.

NOTES:

Section Seven: Pulling it All Together

Roadmap 4.1—Team Building and Talent Acquisition (page 170)

How will you communicate your expectations to your team?

```
┌─────────────────────────────────────────────────────┐
│  OUTCOME:                                           │
│                                                     │
│                                                     │
└─────────────────────────────────────────────────────┘
```

```
┌─────────────────────────────────────────────────────┐
│  STRATEGIES / ACTIVITIES:                           │
│                                                     │
│                                                     │
│                                                     │
│                                                     │
└─────────────────────────────────────────────────────┘
```

```
┌─────────────────────────────────────────────────────┐
│  DATA NEEDED:                                       │
│                                                     │
│                                                     │
│                                                     │
└─────────────────────────────────────────────────────┘
```

```
┌─────────────────────────────────────────────────────┐
│  WHOM TO INVOLVE:                                   │
│                                                     │
│                                                     │
│                                                     │
└─────────────────────────────────────────────────────┘
```

Section Seven: Pulling it All Together

COMMUNICATION NEEDED (BETTER MODALITIES):

WHEN (TIMING: SPECIFIC WEEK/MONTH):

PRIORITY RANKING:

Checklist—Items to Do Next:

To continue assessing your team members:

√ Gather secondary data, such as CVs and position descriptions.

√ Ask the communications office for an expertise list and review it.

ROADMAP 4.2—IDENTIFYING SKILLS AND COMPETENCIES IN BUILDING YOUR TEAM (PAGE 185)

How are you going to assess the professional development needs of people in your unit?

OUTCOME:

STRATEGIES / ACTIVITIES:

DATA NEEDED:

Section Seven: Pulling it All Together

WHOM TO INVOLVE:

COMMUNICATION NEEDED (BETTER MODALITIES):

WHEN (TIMING: SPECIFIC WEEK/MONTH):

PRIORITY RANKING:

4.2 CONTINUED. Develop a plan for providing for professional development needs that you identify in your unit. Think especially about low-cost ways to meet these needs over the next 1-2 years.

OUTCOME:

STRATEGIES / ACTIVITIES:

DATA NEEDED:

Section Seven: Pulling it All Together

WHOM TO INVOLVE:

COMMUNICATION NEEDED (BETTER MODALITIES):

WHEN (TIMING: SPECIFIC WEEK/MONTH):

PRIORITY RANKING:

Roadmap 5.1—Creating or Reinforcing a Culture of Data-Supported Decision Making (page 209)

Checklist—Items to Do First:

√ Inquire about and join your institution's data governance and/or data analytics council.

Next, determine: What data sources exist for your unit and the campus?

OUTCOME:

STRATEGIES / ACTIVITIES:

DATA NEEDED:

Section Seven: Pulling it All Together

WHOM TO INVOLVE:

COMMUNICATION NEEDED (BETTER MODALITIES):

WHEN (TIMING: SPECIFIC WEEK/MONTH):

PRIORITY RANKING:

5.1 CONTINUED. Plan ongoing training for your team members to make routine and strategic decisions with data.

OUTCOME:

STRATEGIES / ACTIVITIES:

DATA NEEDED:

Section Seven: Pulling it All Together

WHOM TO INVOLVE:

COMMUNICATION NEEDED (BETTER MODALITIES):

WHEN (TIMING: SPECIFIC WEEK/MONTH):

PRIORITY RANKING:

5.1 CONTINUED. Plan to hold unit-level "Data Days" to review and update data and encourage the use of data to make decisions:

OUTCOME:

STRATEGIES / ACTIVITIES:

DATA NEEDED:

Section Seven: Pulling it All Together

WHOM TO INVOLVE:

COMMUNICATION NEEDED (BETTER MODALITIES):

WHEN (TIMING: SPECIFIC WEEK/MONTH):

PRIORITY RANKING:

Roadmap 5.2—Budget and Resource Allocation (page 223)

Calculate the return on investment or value-added for your unit.

OUTCOME:

STRATEGIES / ACTIVITIES:

DATA NEEDED:

Section Seven: Pulling it All Together

WHOM TO INVOLVE:

COMMUNICATION NEEDED (BETTER MODALITIES):

WHEN (TIMING: SPECIFIC WEEK/MONTH):

PRIORITY RANKING:

5.2 CONTINUED. Make a plan to align your budget to your priorities.

OUTCOME:

STRATEGIES / ACTIVITIES:

DATA NEEDED:

Section Seven: Pulling it All Together

WHOM TO INVOLVE:

COMMUNICATION NEEDED (BETTER MODALITIES):

WHEN (TIMING: SPECIFIC WEEK/MONTH):

PRIORITY RANKING:

5.2 CONTINUED. After aligning your budget and priorities, determine if you need more resources and make a plan to request them.

OUTCOME:

STRATEGIES / ACTIVITIES:

DATA NEEDED:

Section Seven: Pulling it All Together

WHOM TO INVOLVE:

COMMUNICATION NEEDED (BETTER MODALITIES):

WHEN (TIMING: SPECIFIC WEEK/MONTH):

PRIORITY RANKING:

Roadmap 5.3—Assessment and Accreditation (page 237)

Checklist—Items to Do First:

√ Obtain a calendar of accreditations and determine: Do you or your unit have a role?

√ Review your unit's goals to ensure they align with institutional goals.

Next, look for areas of improvement that are often mentioned repeatedly in assessments/accreditations/evaluations but which remain unaddressed. Determine who should be responsible for 'fixing' them and, if they fall under your portfolio, delegate.

OUTCOME:

STRATEGIES / ACTIVITIES:

DATA NEEDED:

Section Seven: Pulling It All Together

WHOM TO INVOLVE:

COMMUNICATION NEEDED (BETTER MODALITIES):

WHEN (TIMING: SPECIFIC WEEK/MONTH):

PRIORITY RANKING:

ROADMAP 5.4—INTERSECTING PURVIEWS (PAGE 248)

CHECKLIST—ITEMS TO DO FIRST:

√ Assess what your team knows about finance and budgeting—and establish training and updates for your unit.

Then, if you have identified gaps while completing the microcontext in Section 4.2, develop a consultation documentation process. Make sure to:

- Require written consultation documents that consider more than allocation increases for their units.
- Require the inclusion of efficiency plans and resource reallocation plans that align with key performance indicators and strategic goals.

OUTCOME:

STRATEGIES / ACTIVITIES:

DATA NEEDED:

Section Seven: Pulling it All Together

WHOM TO INVOLVE:

COMMUNICATION NEEDED (BETTER MODALITIES):

WHEN (TIMING: SPECIFIC WEEK/MONTH):

PRIORITY RANKING:

5.4 CONTINUED. If you have identified gaps while completing the microcontext in Section 4.2, develop a written process for requesting positions.

OUTCOME:

STRATEGIES / ACTIVITIES:

DATA NEEDED:

Section Seven: Pulling it All Together

WHOM TO INVOLVE:

COMMUNICATION NEEDED (BETTER MODALITIES):

WHEN (TIMING: SPECIFIC WEEK/MONTH):

PRIORITY RANKING:

ROADMAP 6.2—REVIEW OF POLICIES AND PRACTICES (PAGE 273)

CHECKLIST—ITEMS TO DO FIRST:

√ Review policies in light of the function of your unit, your goals and objectives, human and financial resources, and external operating environment.

√ Review policies before taking a job or soon after arriving on campus. Otherwise, you may default to operating under the policies of your previous institution.

√ Inquire about the last time policies were audited for alignment with your unit's goals and objectives.

Then, develop a plan for adding or revising policies, as needed:

OUTCOME:

STRATEGIES / ACTIVITIES:

DATA NEEDED:

Section Seven: Pulling it All Together

WHOM TO INVOLVE:

COMMUNICATION NEEDED (BETTER MODALITIES):

WHEN (TIMING: SPECIFIC WEEK/MONTH):

PRIORITY RANKING:

APPENDIX: CAST OF CHARACTERS AT JACKSON ROCKGROVE UNIVERSITY

> **JRU MISSION**
>
> - We develop responsible citizens and leaders through inclusive educational opportunities.
>
> **JRU VALUES**
>
> - Excellence
> - Diversity
> - Community engagement
> - Global perspective
> - Service
> - Sustainability

Case Study Characters (In Order of Introduction)

Central administration

FRANKIE FISCAL. Chief Financial Officer. At the institution for 15 years; newly promoted to CFO from within.

MONA VOLADOR. Human Resources Director. Has spent their career at this institution, starting at secretary. Promoted to the role rather than selected through a search process. Does not have any formal education in HR.

Appendix

Provost Earnest. In office for six months. Previously served long term as a department chair and has been dean at two different institutions.

President Petry. In office for three years; very concerned with appearances and popularity; doesn't want to make anyone mad. Lives in fear of a vote of no confidence, especially based on campus racial climate issues.

(Former) Provost Pretentious. Now a university president at another institution, Pretentious used their time as provost to create a portfolio of accomplishments to help achieve that position.

(Former) President Paternal. President for 25 years prior to retirement. Longest-serving president in JRU history. Friends with Big Bucks Bentley and other longtime members of the university community.

Tanner True. Associate Provost. Well-respected, former chair of the science department for many years, recently hired to serve in this role after a national search.

Newby Nelson. Vice President of Student Success. Newby's purview includes student affairs, enrollment management, and advancement. They are new to the campus.

Deans

Dean Jolly. In their second 3-year term as dean. Jovial, but allergic to conflict—or work.

Dean Wink. Was promoted from within about three years ago after serving as chair of a very successful and prestigious department. Has a history of being very friendly and flirty toward colleagues.

Dean Outsider. Second year in the role; served as dean at another institution before coming to this current position.

Dean Perfect. Retired dean who previously presided over Outsider's current college. Perfect returned to the faculty and keeps a low profile.

Dean Lackey. Serving as dean for approximately eight years, Dean Lackey's strategy for keeping their job is to maintain the goodwill of the college faculty at almost all costs.

Staff

Drew Drama. Relative of Big Bucks Bentley; floating employee, has reported to six areas over ten years.

Stevie Staff. Comptroller, reports to Frankie Fiscal. President of Staff Senate for several terms.

Andy Administrator. Oversees Institutional Research, reports to Tanner True.

Remmy Reserved. Introvert with analytical skills; initially served as director of advancement analytics and reported to Newby Nelson; now serving in the newly created role of Chief Data Officer and reports to the president.

Sydney Suckup. A director who has presidential ambitions.

Cameron Candid. Institutional Research. Senior data specialist in the institutional research office; a long-term, well-liked staff member who has limited statistical analytic skills; taking accounting classes.

Coach Southpaw Sanders. Baseball coach and former pitcher for the St. Louis Cardinals. Promoted to athletic director after retirement of the previous athletic director.

AD Duncan. Former athletic director, retired after 15 years in the position. Had an easygoing, informal leadership style.

Max Myway. Assistant athletic director for academic advising. Wants to continue with business as usual after the new athletic director is appointed.

Faculty

Professor Combative. Very limited, poor scholarship with marginal teaching performance. Hired six years ago.

Tricky Dick. Full professor in history, tenured, a prolific scholar who refuses to engage in service, such as serving as department chair.

Blake. Postdoc fellow in their first year at JRU.

Trusting Taylor. Associate professor in history, tenured for one year. Called to do a lot of service to compensate for the fact that there are few full-time faculty in the department.

Dr. Alex Assistant. Junior faculty, not tenured; in their second year at the institution.

Dr. Abby Monkson. Senate president; associate professor, co-led program review process, served on the Faculty Senate for 12 years; second term as Senate president.

Dr. Harper Hustle. Full professor in the science department.

Dr. Pat Pompous. Department chair, associate professor, former Senate leader, co-led program review process; in an accredited program that allows for multiple releases for their administration time.

Appendix

Professor Singer. MFA, associate professor, tenured; in their third term as chair of the music department.

Dr. Dogma. Associate professor, worked at institution for 25 years, started as an adjunct, and earned doctorate eight years ago; newly tenured.

Professor Mensch. Associate professor, well-rounded campus citizen in teaching (excellent), scholarship, (prolific), service (does as asked).

Murphy Meager. ABD (adjunct); has vacillated between temporary full-time and adjunct appointments for two years at the institution. Has been working on their dissertation for five years.

Dr. Dissatisfied. Tenured, associate professor, at institution for 25 years. Never elected to leadership or appointed to interim administrative roles, even though they wanted these roles.

Community members

Big Bucks Bentley. Donor/alum/trustee. Has multiple endowments at institution; MBA from the institution; owns a large regional company.

ABOUT THE AUTHORS

Maria Thompson, Ph.D.

President and CEO, Retired, Coppin State University

Maria is a career educator whose work experience spans a variety of institutional categories, including research universities, comprehensive universities, land-grant universities, urban-located, rural-located HBCUs, and PWIs. She was president and CEO of Coppin State University (CSU), provost and vice president for academic affairs at the State University of New York (SUNY), and vice president for research and sponsored programs at Tennessee State University. Maria earned her Bachelor of Science degree from Tennessee State University, a Master of Science degree from the Ohio State University, and a doctorate from the University of Tennessee, Knoxville.

Susan C. Turell, Ph.D.

Former Provost, Marywood University

In higher education for 29 years, Susan brings a passion to her work for supporting people and designing and implementing effective processes. She served in leadership as a department chair, associate provost, dean, and provost. She brings those experiences, as well as her training and practice as a psychologist, to synthesize best practices and approaches in a new paradigm about what it means to be an effective leader in 21st century higher education. A seasoned administrator who is a teacher at heart, Susan welcomes the opportunity to share her learnings with new and aspiring leaders to strengthen their leadership skills, encourage their optimism, and support their vision for new possibilities. Susan earned her Ph.D. and M.Ed. in Counseling Psychology from the University of Houston, and her B.A. in Plan II (Honors Program) from the University of Texas-Austin. She has worked at regional comprehensive universities in both large and small state systems, and at a private religious university.

Made in the USA
Las Vegas, NV
02 June 2022